BERRYMAN AND LOWELL:
THE ART OF LOSING

Berryman and Lowell

The Art of Losing

Stephen Matterson

BARNES & NOBLE BOOKS
TOTOWA, NEW JERSEY

© Stephen John Matterson 1988

First published in the USA 1988 by
BARNES & NOBLE BOOKS
81 ADAMS DRIVE
TOTOWA, NEW JERSEY, 07512

Library of Congress Cataloging-in-Publication Data
Matterson, Stephen.
Berryman and Lowell: the art of losing.
Bibliography: p.
Includes index.
1. American poetry—20th century—History and
criticism.   2. Berryman, John, 1914–1972—Criticism and
interpretation.   3. Lowell, Robert, 1917–1977—Criticism
and interpretation.   4. Loss (Psychology) in literature.
I. Title.
PS323.5.M38 1988   811'.5'09   87–1824
ISBN 0–389–20730–6

For Jean
with all of my love

Contents

Contents

Acknowledgements

I should like to thank Frances Arnold, my editor at Macmillan, and the outside reader whose advice and comments helped to shape the book. For special help and encouragement, I am personally grateful to Ray Cowell, Jean Nee, Mike Scott, Larry Vonalt and John Wakeley.

Grateful acknowledgement is made to copyright holders for permission to quote the following: 'The Ball Poem' and excerpts from 'Winter Landscape', 'Young Woman's Song', and 'The Statue' from *Short Poems* and *Homage to Mistress Bradstreet* by John Berryman. Copyright © 1940, 1946 by John Berryman. Copyright Renewed © 1968 by John Berryman. Excerpts from *His Toy, His Dream, His Rest* by John Berryman. Copyright © 1964, 1965, 1966, 1967, 1968 by John Berryman. Excerpt from *Love & Fame* by John Berryman. Copyright © 1970 by John Berryman. Excerpt from 'The Facts and Issues' from *Delusions Etc.* by John Berryman. Copyright © 1969, 1971 by John Berryman. Copyright © 1972 by the Estate of John Berryman. Reprinted by permission of Farrar, Straus and Giroux, Inc., and by permission of Faber and Faber Ltd.

Excerpts from the unpublished notebooks and letters of John Berryman are taken from the John Berryman Collection, University of Minnesota, and from The Houghton Library, Harvard University. They are reprinted by permission of Kate Donahue, literary executrix of the estate of John Berryman, Al Lathrop, curator of the John Berryman Collection and joint executor of the estate of John Berryman, and by permission of The Houghton Library.

Excerpts from 'As a Plane Tree by the Water', 'Colloquy in Black Rock', 'The Quaker Graveyard in Nantucket', 'In Memory of Arthur Winslow', from *Lord Weary's Castle* and *Poems 1938–49* by Robert Lowell. Copyright © 1946, 1974 by Robert Lowell. Reprinted by permission of Harcourt, Brace, Jovanovich, Inc., and by permission of Faber and Faber Ltd. Excerpts from 'The Mills of the Kavanaughs', 'Mother Marie Therese', from *The Mills of the Kavanaughs* and *Poems 1938–49* by Robert Lowell. Copyright © 1951 by Robert Lowell; renewed 1979 by Harriet W. Lowell. Reprinted by permission of Harcourt, Brace, Jovanovich, Inc., and Faber and Faber Ltd.

'Father's Bedroom', excerpts from 'Inauguration Day, 1953',

'Beyond the Alps', 'The Banker's Daughter', from *Life Studies* by Robert Lowell. Copyright © 1956, 1959 by Robert Lowell. 'Reading Myself', 'The Nihilist as Hero', 'For John Berryman 1', 'End of a Year' from *History* by Robert Lowell. Copyright © 1967, 1968, 1969, 1970, 1973 by Robert Lowell. Excerpt from 'Fishnet', from *The Dolphin* by Robert Lowell. Copyright © 1973 by Robert Lowell. Excerpts from 'For John Berryman', 'Grass Fires', 'Epilogue', 'Wellesley Free', 'Turtle', 'Fetus', 'Unwanted' from *Day by Day* by Robert Lowell. Copyright © 1975, 1976, 1977 by Robert Lowell. Reprinted by permission of Farrar, Straus and Giroux, Inc., and by permission of Faber and Faber Ltd.

Excerpts from Robert Lowell's letters are taken from the John Berryman Collection, University of Minnesota, and are reprinted by permission of the Estate of Robert Lowell and Farrar Straus and Giroux, Inc.

'My Papa's Waltz' from *The Collected Poems of Theodore Roethke* by Theodore Roethke, copyright © 1942 by Hearst Magazines Inc., reprinted by permission of Doubleday and Company Inc., and by permission of Faber and Faber Ltd.

'Men Made Out of Words' from *The Collected Poems of Wallace Stevens* by Wallace Stevens. Copyright © Wallace Stevens 1954. Reprinted by permission of Alfred A. Knopf, Inc., and by permission of Faber and Faber Ltd.

Stephen Matterson

Chronologies

1968   *His Toy, His Dream, His Rest*
1969   National Book Award and Bollingen Prize awarded for *His*
         Toy, His Dream, His Rest
         Single volume edition of *The Dream Songs*
         Appointed Regents' Professor, University of Minnesota
1970   Treatment for alcoholism
         Love & Fame
1971   British, revised, version of *Love & Fame*
         Second daughter, Sarah, born
1972   Suicide, 7 January, Minneapolis

Posthumous Publications

1972   *Delusions Etc. Selected Poems 1938–1968*
1973   *Recovery* (novel)
1976   *The Freedom of the Poet* (critical essays and short stories)
1977   *Henry's Fate & Other Poems 1967–1972* (ed. John Haffenden)

ROBERT LOWELL

1917   Born 1 March, Boston
1935–7   Attended Harvard University
1937–40   Attended Kenyon College, Ohio
1940   Became Roman Catholic
          Married Jean Stafford
1940–1   Taught at Kenyon
          Graduate study, Louisiana State University
1943   Imprisoned for violation of Selective Service Act
1944   Living Maine, New York
          Land of Unlikeness
1946   *Lord Weary's Castle*
1947   Pulitzer Prize awarded for *Lord Weary's Castle*
1948   Divorced from Jean Stafford
1949   In hospital; beginning of recurrent mental disturbances
          Married to Elizabeth Hardwick
1950–3   Living in Europe
1950   *Poems 1938–1949*
1951   *The Mills of the Kavanaughs*
          Wins Harriet Monroe Poetry Prize
1954–60   Living in Boston, teaches at Boston University
1957   Birth of daughter, Harriet

1959   *Life Studies*
        Wins National Book Award
1961   *Imitations* (wins Bollingen Translation Prize)
        Figaro (with Jacques Barzun). *Phaedra*
1963–77 Teaching regularly at Harvard University
1964   *For the Union Dead*
        The Old Glory (trilogy of plays); wins Obie award
1967   *Near the Ocean*
1968   Revised version of *The Old Glory*
1969   *Notebook 1967–68*
        Prometheus Bound (play)
1970   *Notebook*
1970–6 Living in England, teaching at Harvard one semester a
        year. Taught at All Souls College, Oxford (1970); Essex
        University (1970–2).
1971   Son, Robert Sheridan, born to Lowell and Caroline
        Blackwood
1972   Divorced from Elizabeth Hardwick; married to Caroline
        Blackwood
1973   *The Dolphin* (wins Pulitzer Prize)
        History
        For Lizzie and Harriet
1974   *Robert Lowell's Poems: A Selection* (ed. Jonathan Raban)
1976   *Selected Poems*
1977   *Day by Day* (won National Book Critics Circle Award)
        Revised edition of *Selected Poems*
        Death, New York, 12 September

Posthumous Publication

1978   *The Oresteia of Aeschylus*

What should we be without the sexual myth,
The human reverie or poem of death?

Castratos of moon-mash – Life consists
Of propositions about life. The human

Reverie is a solitude in which
We compose these propositions, torn by dreams,

By the terrible incantations of defeats
And by the fear that defeats and dreams are one.

The whole race is a poet that writes down
The eccentric propositions of its fate.

Wallace Stevens

Introduction: Tumbles and Leaps

What queer lives we've had even for poets! There seems something generic about it, and determined beyond anything we could do. You and I have had so many of the same tumbles and leaps. . . .

(Lowell to Berryman, 1962)

Robert Lowell and John Berryman were the foremost members of what is now generally called the 'middle generation' of twentieth-century American poets. Even in the generation which included poets such as Elizabeth Bishop, Delmore Schwartz, Randall Jarrell and Theodore Roethke, Lowell and Berryman were outstanding. Although they never collaborated, their achievement was, in many respects, a joint one. Their generation grew up poetically dominated by Eliot, Pound and Yeats. Since these central figures of modernist poetry exerted so tremendous an influence on successive poets, it seemed inevitable that those seeking a style in the 1930s and 1940s would learn from modernism, writing in the styles that the modernists made familiar.

It can plausibly be argued that the fault in the work of Schwartz and Roethke was due to their inability to wrestle with and overcome forces and influences which threatened them. Roethke in particular has become almost a model of how a poet can be overwhelmed by the influence of precursor poets. From his first book, he conceded the problem of creating a space for poetic individuality when confronted with the supremacy of earlier poets. He saw himself in a state of feud with the past, dreading the 'menace of ancestral eyes':

> This ancient feud
> Is seldom won. The spirit starves
> Until the dead have been subdued.

('Feud')

This sense of feud was a problem that each of the middle generation had to confront. Roethke was eventually to accept influence rather than struggle against it. Instead of struggling with, say, Donne, Wordsworth, Yeats and Eliot, or seeking a space elsewhere for his own originality, he claimed that his own poetry disturbed the very idea of originality. He sought poetic interaction with these and other poets, implying that he was in this way continuing the tradition that they embodied.

Roethke wrote about poetic influence with articulate insight, notably in the essay 'How to Write like Somebody Else'. But there is a sense of defeat in the argument itself, as there is in Delmore Schwartz's submission that Roethke's imitations are essentially creative.[1] Berryman and Lowell were clearly dissatisfied with acceptance or imitation of poetic forebears. They wrestled continually with these poetic father figures. During the 1950s both men developed styles and voices distinctly individual. In 1955 Berryman, having already written *Homage to Mistress Bradstreet* (1953) began the Dream Songs. In 1959 Lowell published *Life Studies*. The Dream Songs (*77 Dream Songs* was published in 1964 and *His Toy, His Dream, His Rest* in 1968) and *Life Studies* are astonishing poems. Here only two of their significant features need to be emphasised. *Life Studies* and the sequence of Dream Songs clearly signalled a radical departure from the influence of Eliot and Yeats. In developing their own voices Lowell and Berryman came in turn to lead a fresh group of poets. This group or generation has been given several names, some of which, like the 'confessional poets', are misleading. One idea is that Lowell and Berryman have been the first 'postmodernist' poets; a view put forward by very different critics. Thus Allan Rodway, searching around for the start of postmodernism, wrote that it seemed to have started in the 'anguished personal confession' of Berryman and Lowell.[2] In his controversial introduction to *The New Poetry* Al Alvarez hailed Berryman and Lowell as the first American poets to assimilate the influence of Eliot and then move away from it.[3] In *Enlarging The Temple* Charles Altieri is firm in his choice of Lowell as the poet who introduced 'specific postmodern modes of articulating new values'.[4]

Caution ought certainly to be recommended when dealing with the terms 'modern' and 'postmodern', since they imply that different ideas and techniques may be very neatly polarised. It is nevertheless true that once they developed their own highly individual voices Lowell and Berryman seemed to be radically changed poets. One could call their later styles postmodernist in a simply chronological sense, but this also suggests how their individuality had been achieved through struggle with modernist voices. How Berryman and Lowell achieved those individual styles, and what characteristics those styles shared, are very much the themes of this book.

At several points in the correspondence between Berryman and Lowell it was suggested that the similarities of their lives made up a 'generic' life. The phrase is Lowell's, used in the poem written after Berryman's death; 'Yet really we had the same life, / the generic one / our generation offered.'[5] Indeed, as Lowell implies, this model of a 'generic life' applied to other members of the middle generation. Parental difficulties in childhood, severe emotional strain, alcoholism, depression and mental illness are among the now familiar features of this model. Randall Jarrell's parents were divorced when he was a child and he was raised by his grandparents. When she was aged only eight months Elizabeth Bishop's father died. Her mother, after fits of insanity, was committed permanently to an institution: Bishop never saw her after the age of five. Schwartz's father abandoned the family when Delmore was nine. Lowell's father was dominated by his wife to the extent that he appeared ineffectual. When Berryman was aged eleven his father committed suicide. His mother remarried a little later. (Berryman's name had been John Allyn Smith: on his mother's remarriage he was legally adopted by his mother's new husband and his name became John Allyn McAlpin Berryman.) The title of Roethke's book *The Lost Son* (1948) could be an appropriate title for these members of the middle generation. Indeed, that title might be aptly used to indicate the themes of *Life Studies*, the Dream Songs, Schwartz's *Genesis* and Jarrell's *The Lost World*. The middle generation were lost or deserted children. For them, and for Lowell and Berryman particularly, the need for parents came to be closely involved with the search for a poetic father.

The Lowell and Berryman families were dominated by the mothers. Lowell's mother was a strong-willed woman – in Lowell's account (in '91 Revere Street') it is she who makes the decisions, bullying the in any case rather submissive father. Berryman's mother apparently lavished her affection (and ambition) on him: later in life he was to feel considerably stifled by her love for him. In a highly ambiguous movement, Lowell both recognised and resisted an association with Berryman in this area:

I read an article on a friend
as if recognizing my obituary:
"Though his mother loved her son consumingly,
she lacked a really affectionate nature;
so he always loved what he missed."
That was John Berryman's mother, not mine.[6]

If both poets were 'lost sons', the loss was in Berryman's case acutely real. Thus a continuing theme in the Dream Songs is the abandonment that a father's suicide represents. His adoptive father, John Angus Berryman, is depicted by John Haffenden as a mild, unremarkable figure.[7] Ian Hamilton presents Lowell's father similarly; meek, submissive, mild-mannered.[8] *Life Studies* does focus on the weaknesses of R. T. S. Lowell, suggesting that the loss which both Berryman and Lowell felt in the lack of a father became incorporated into a much larger sense of loss.

Most critics of Berryman and Lowell have suggested that in the 1930s both men were searching for acceptable poetic fathers. For Lowell this search may be linked to a sense of the inadequacies of his real father. In 1936 Lowell knocked his father down in a quarrel. To Lowell this seemed a crucial incident, and one to which he returned several times in his work. His parents sought psychiatric help for their son, and he thus began to visit Merrill Moore. As it happened, Moore had been a member of the 'Fugitives' during the 1920s. This celebrated group of Southern writers based in Nashville had included, among others, John Crowe Ransom, Allen Tate, Donald Davidson and Robert Penn Warren. Moore's advice to Lowell was to visit Tate. Coincidentally, around this time Lowell met Ford Madox Ford; his advice was the same as Moore's: go South, and meet Tate. Lowell did so. In the late 1950s Lowell wrote lightly of his 1937 visit to the Tates. But the serious fact was that Tate became Lowell's poetic father, to the extent that Lowell even began to address him as 'father' – much to Tate's discomfort.[9] The ideas of Tate and of Ransom were to help Lowell find a style and to develop particular themes and attitudes. He once said that his early poetry was 'studded with Eliot'; but it is also full of the ideas of Tate and Ransom.[10] Indeed, in a 1947 letter, Roethke wrote that Lowell was too heavily influenced by Tate. However, Tate also served Jarrell and Roethke as a poetic guide. Roethke's great respect for Tate comes over again and again in the *Selected Letters*. Jarrell's *Blood for a Stranger* (1942) was dedicated to him.

While Lowell was thus 'visiting the Tates', Berryman was intent upon his own quest. In 1936 he had won a scholarship enabling him to study at Clare College, Cambridge. A strong incentive for Berryman was the chance to meet Yeats, and he did so in 1937. Looking back at his early work, Berryman tended to regard himself rather wryly:

> I began work in verse-making as a burning, trivial disciple of the great Irish poet William Butler Yeats . . . whom I didn't so much wish to resemble as to *be*.[11]

Lowell's early work showed a great deal more merit than that of Jarrell, Berryman and Roethke. Indeed, the impact of *Lord Weary's Castle* was nearly as powerful as that of Schwartz's first book, *In Dreams Begin Responsibilities* (1938). *Lord Weary's Castle* earned a Pulitzer prize for Lowell. His Roman Catholicism gave Lowell a very particular thematic sense of direction, and technically he was a great deal more assured than Berryman. But his loss of faith ultimately meant rejection of his earlier themes and style. *The Mills of the Kavanaughs* (1951) was Lowell's important failure, leading him eventually to *Life Studies*. Berryman, however, had been developing more gradually, and the style that can be considered his own began in several poems of *The Dispossessed* (1948). *Homage to Mistress Bradstreet* firmly established Berryman's own voice, leading him also to be considered a major poet.

These developments, though, involved serious breaks with the established poetic fathers. Tate was said to be 'horrified' by *Life Studies*, and tried to persuade Lowell not to publish it.[12] *Homage to Mistress Bradstreet* departed wholly from the Yeatsian poetic that Berryman had carefully fostered in his earlier work. It was also the poem with which Berryman sought explicitly to evade the influence of T. S. Eliot:

> let us have something spectacularly NOT *The Waste Land*, the best long poem of the age. So maybe hostility keeps us going.[13]

This 'hostility', this capacity to break away from their established styles, sharply distinguishes Berryman and Lowell from other members of the middle generation. Roethke's work shows clear and strong lines of development. But it is not development away from his established influences. He moves closer and closer to others, his work becoming an interaction with that of past great poets, notably Yeats. The rich achievement of Roethke's last books is undeniable. But it is a dependent richness. Jarrell and Bishop also do not follow the paths that Lowell and Berryman took, the striking away from poetic influence. This is largely because Jarrell and Bishop were from the start quite individual poets. They stand outside the mainstream of mid-twentieth-century writing, uncommitted to any particular school. As such, their work shows only small development. Both grew more assured, more certain: Bishop in particular has made a kind of poetry uniquely hers. If their work does not have the power of that by Berryman and Lowell, it is partly because they lacked such specific energies. 'Maybe hostility keeps us going', wrote Berryman. For him and Lowell it was true. Their need to break from strong influence eventually formed a source of tremendous energy, a fund for further development. The distance that Jarrell and Bishop had maintained from influences perhaps deprived them of such energy, made such a source unavailable to them. They had no need of the hostility that Berryman and Lowell required: their achievement was already well defined as their own.

In the 1960s Berryman and Lowell consolidated their recently established modes while moving further into new areas. If Elizabeth Bishop is momentarily excluded from the group, the middle generation shared a variety of crucially similar life experiences. Schwartz's isolation and paranoia correspond to the mental breakdowns of Roethke, Lowell and Jarrell, to the guilt and fears of Berryman. Alcoholism is another prominent feature of the group, as is marital difficulty. While such experiences may seem randomly shared, they have contributed much to our sense of a generic life. Also, the pain and suffering evident in their lives and articulated in their poetry have contributed similarly to an overall sense of the contemporary position of the poet.

Berryman and Lowell were both to use the long poem. It is likely that Berryman's future reputation will rest on the Dream Songs, but Lowell's 1973 collection, *History* (preceded as it was by *Notebook 1967–68* and *Notebook*), has failed to receive the wide critical acclaim given to *Life Studies, For the Union Dead* (1964) and *Near the Ocean* (1967). However, analysis of the important similarities between *History* and the Dream Songs assists our appreciation of both works. Finally, the last works of both poets have taken some time to receive positive critical appraisal. The short personal 'reminiscences' of *Love & Fame* (1970) may be compared with Lowell's last poems, in *Day by*

Day (1977). Along with Berryman's *Delusions Etc* (1972), these books lack the intensity and rhetorical stylisation for which Lowell and Berryman were renowned. Readers of Berryman and Lowell have also had trouble assimilating these books into the respective canons. In their final works both poets had once again changed from a recently established style.

The similar patterns of their lives ought not to imply, even accidentally, any striking personal closeness between Berryman and Lowell. Their written correspondence was irregular, often with long gaps between letters. However, they deeply admired one another's work, and in their feelings towards each other a strong sense of rivalry was also present. Rivalry combined with mutual admiration is a notable feature of these middle generation poets: it is certainly not exclusive to Berryman and Lowell. However, their well-known rivalry and the idea of a generic life produced the joke in an otherwise insensitive rumour that circulated in New York City after Berryman's suicide. It was well known that Berryman had left no suicide note: the rumour (started, it has been suggested, by W. H. Auden) was that he did, and it read 'Your move, Cal'.[14]

Both men wrote with acute perception about the other's work. Berryman's rightly celebrated essay on 'Skunk Hour', entitled 'Despondency and Madness', won high praise from Lowell. In a letter to Berryman he wrote that the very accuracy of Berryman's comments and insights had made him uncomfortable:

. . . you've made an amazing guess, more or less a bull's-eye thrust into what was going on when the poem was written – all very dazzling and disturbing.[15]

In his published comments on the essay Lowell once more remarked on how disturbing Berryman's reading had been. However, in the letter he goes on to suggest that Berryman could be so accurate about the poem because of their shared experiences and perspective: 'I feel we are very close and see things with the same mixture of cheerfullness [*sic*] and sourness. . . .' Lowell returned to this idea on several occasions. Not surprisingly, perhaps, one can see that the Berryman poems which he most admired were those closest to his own interests and concerns. In the *New York Review of Books* Lowell distinguished certain features of Berryman's work, and in doing so highlighted his own interests. Thus he considered *Homage to Mistress Bradstreet* 'the most resourceful historical poem in our literature'.[16] Although he praised *77 Dream Songs*, he found it a 'hazardous, imperfect book': a criticism very close to those which would later be made of *Notebook* and *History*. In fact, Berryman privately felt that Lowell's *Notebook* was in part an attempt to imitate the success of the Dream Songs.[17] In a letter of 1968, Lowell briefly outlined the similarities between *Notebook* and the Dream Songs: in a postscript he also enumerated what he saw as the differences.

Although aware of the difficulties of the Dream Songs, Lowell greatly admired the sequence, choosing the Opus Posthumous songs for special praise. Shortly after reading them for the first time (they are Dream Songs 78–91) Lowell sent a cable to Berryman: 'Your posthumous poems are a tremendous and living triumph Love Cal'.[18] A little later he wrote in detail:

> The Opus posth. poems seem to me the crown of your wonderful work, witty, heart-breaking, all of a piece . . . Somehow one believes you on this huge matter of looking at death and your whole life. I'm sure it will be read on and on, one of the lovely things in our literature.[19]

Undoubtedly, such praise and encouragement meant a great deal to Berryman, who had published the first book of Dream Songs partly on Lowell's suggestion. Several years later, Lowell's admiration helped Berryman considerably during a time of serious self-doubt. Although Berryman was deeply hurt by attacks on *Love & Fame*, attacks which he considered the result of critical misunderstanding, Lowell's praise of 'Eleven Addresses to the Lord' was lavish:

> I've read your marvelous prayer at the end of your book, and can hardly find words to praise it. . . . Anyway, it's one of the great poems of the age, a puzzle and a triumph to anyone who wants to write a personal devotional poem. Along with your posthumous poems, to my mind, the crown of your work.[20]

Such enthusiasm restored Berryman's self-esteem, offsetting both the poor reception of *Love & Fame* and a crushing personal attack in a letter from Allen Tate. His own admiration for Lowell's work was constant. He took great pride in having worked with Lowell on the proofs of *Lord Weary's Castle*, even offering some amendments to 'The Quaker Graveyard in Nantucket'.[21] It was after Berryman's urging that Lowell restored the third stanza of 'Beyond the Alps', cut from the first edition of *Life Studies*. With Berryman, though, personal gratitude was usually included in his admiration of Lowell, as in this slightly exaggerated account from a letter to an unidentified correspondent:

> Two of the men I feel most grateful to . . . are Saul [Bellow] and Cal Lowell . . . I try to remember that I kept him in Maine on the proofs of *Lord Weary* fifteen years ago and helped make his American reputation w. an endless review in *Partisan* and held his hand many times, between marriages (his and mine), in New York, and when he was going out, and just did a living essay . . . on his 'Skunk Hour'.[22]

For all their mutual admiration, the rivalry between the two men is difficult to ignore. It seems to have been felt most keenly by Berryman, probably because Lowell was a major poet for such a long time. Fame came to Lowell early and stayed with him to the end of his life. Berryman achieved recognition comparatively late. All the longing for prominence in the first parts of *Love & Fame* had a firm basis in reality. Daniel Hughes once recalled being with Berryman on the day that Frost died. Given the news, Berryman's reaction was to ask 'Who's number one? Who's number one? Cal is number one, isn't he?'[23] Nevertheless, Berryman had an acute awareness of Lowell's superiority: in a letter to Lowell he once wrote 'But why publish verse anyway? It's all right for you to do, but why the rest of us?'[24] Lowell himself tended publicly to play down the idea of rivalry between poets, but John Thompson wrote that Lowell had other poets 'precisely ranked' and that at times this ranking emerged.[25] Perhaps, though, the competition between Berryman and Lowell was actually a major stimulus to their work. If it is after all true that Lowell tried to imitate the success of the Dream Songs with *Notebook* and *History*, we certainly ought not to complain. Berryman remarked that maybe 'hostility' could be one source for discovering individuality. In Dream Song no. 312 he wrote 'ingratitude is the necessary curse / of making things new.' Once Lowell and Berryman had moved outside of the influence of their poetic fathers (through finding hostility towards them), perhaps it was in part their own rivalry that provided a continuing stimulus to originality. After hostility and ingratitude, rivalry itself became the 'necessary curse'.

This stimulus had its source in other rivalries too, but that between Berryman and Lowell was the most prominent, and, for the two poets, the most important.

Most of the ideas outlined in this introduction can be seen in Lowell's *Day by Day* poem 'For John Berryman'. Lowell's sorrow at Berryman's death is heightened, once more, by the evident parallels between their lives:

> I used to want to live
> to avoid your elegy.
> Yet really we had the same life . . .

Lowell also emphasises other aspects of this 'generic' life: the part played, for instance, by women and drink:

> . . . daydreaming to drink at six,
> waiting for the iced fire,
> even the feel of the frosted glass,
> like waiting for a girl . . .
> if you had waited.
> We asked to be obsessed with writing,
> and we were.

The transitions here, between drinking, waiting for a girl and being obsessed with writing, are not as loose or random as they might appear. Berryman in particular was obsessed, with writing and with alcohol. His constant connection of the two ('Whiskey and ink, whiskey and ink') has become by now a renowned feature of the 'generic' life that Lowell here explores. Once Berryman had developed the form and idiom of the Dream Songs he found that the style obsessed him. On several occasions he attempted to end the sequence: in 1965, for example, he said that the poem would be finished within a year and that it would consist of 161 songs.[26] On the manuscript of the song that became number 25, he wrote 'no more this is the END'.[27] Of course it was not the end, since Berryman found that he was unable to stop writing Dream Songs. In 1966, before his year-long visit to Dublin, he felt that the poem was mostly finished. However, the period in Ireland resulted in a fresh flood of songs. Even after the publication of *His Toy, His Dream, His Rest* he was unable to stop writing in his created idiom. In 1970 Richard Kostelanetz wrote of a meeting with Berryman:

As we spoke, Berryman claimed to have abandoned Henry, but on the table next to him was yet another Dream Song. . . . 'Well, . . . mostly I'm through with Henry, but the minute I say that, pains course through me.'[28]

Delmore Schwartz too found it impossible to cease writing – particularly with *Genesis* – but there are important differences. Schwartz was not obsessed with idiom itself, as were Berryman and Lowell. Also, it was the use of memory in *Genesis* which became obsessive, and this obsession with memory was to haunt Schwartz and to make him feel he had lost his creative capacity. In fact, Berryman's obsession with writing Dream Songs created a major difficulty for readers and critics. The sense of thematic order to the poem was never strong for Berryman, and it weakened as the poem grew. William Meredith suggested that Berryman's method was improvisational, in that he would write an individual song and then attempt to fit it in among the existing sequence.[29] The seventh, final, book of songs suffers most from Berryman's inability to stop writing. There, the large number of songs written in Ireland are assimilated poorly into the work: several critics have commented on how this book's lack of structure contrasts sharply with the sense of order provided by the opening books.

Lowell too created problems for readers with his own professed obsession with the fourteen-liners of *Notebook*. In 1969 *Notebook 1967–68* was published. Lowell then made a rearrangement of that book, and expanded it with new poems to make *Notebook*, published in 1970. In his 'Note to the New Edition' Lowell apologised for asking anyone 'to buy this poem twice', adding that he 'couldn't stop writing'. However, Lowell again made revisions and rearrangements, and added further poems, making two separate books published in 1973: *History* and *For Lizzie and Harriet*. His obsession with the fourteen-line form continued, becoming the form of *The Dolphin*, also published in 1973. As with Berryman, Lowell's obsession with a single form made things difficult for any reader expecting a thematically unified sequence. Although his sense of a larger unity is not so improvisational as Berryman's, Lowell did drastically alter the order of these works. At the basis of *History* and the Dream Songs is an obsession with writing itself.

Towards the end of 'For John Berryman' Lowell turns to the differences between the two men:

> Just the other day,
> I discovered how we differ – humor . . .
> even in this last *Dream Song*,
> to mock your catlike flight
> from home and classes –
> to leap from the bridge.

Presumably, the Dream Song referred to here is the incomplete song written shortly before Berryman's suicide and collected in *Henry's Fate*, with the first line 'I didn't. And I didn't Sharp the Spanish blade'. Although Lowell here implies sudden insight into the quality which distinguishes his work from Berryman's, he had long been sensitive to these differences. In a letter of 1968 he considered the similarities between the Dream Songs and his own *Notebook 1967–68*. But he also went on to consider some of the differences:

> Of course, my tone is mine. We both have a good deal of gaiety and desperation; but I would say your world is rather more comic. My universe, my 16 months of time are tragic. . . . Tragic and comic aren't the right words, but you will understand.[30]

As well as these differences in tone, Lowell was keenly aware of their stylistic differences. In 1959 he wrote to Berryman:

> I wonder if you need so much twisting, obscurity, archaisms, strange word orders, &-signs for *and*, etc.? I guess you do. Surely here, as in the Bradstreet, you have your voice. It vibrates and makes the heart ache.[31]

Anyone acquainted with the developed styles of Berryman and Lowell would perceive these differences. The world of Berryman is after all both comic and tragic, his idiom a vital language – 'racy jabber', Lowell called it.[32] For Berryman, Lowell was 'the Bostonian, / rugged & grand & sorrowful'. Humour is certainly rare in Lowell's work, and when it is present it usually includes a rhetorical or serious quality that halts any comic effect. It may be as well here to enumerate other differences between the two poets. In his first books Lowell presents his powerfully-held religious views, and these provide the basis for his first poetic identity. In his early work, though, Berryman is in no sense a religious writer. Also, both men moved from the influence of modernism in different ways.

Though their respective breaks from the modernists possess many common features, they led finally to the development of very different styles. Also, Lowell's poetry often considers major public and political issues. However ambiguous the public stance becomes in *For the Union Dead* and *Near the Ocean*, it is missing from Berryman's poetry. Despite the view that Berryman and Lowell are comparable, they remain very distinctive poets.

It would not be difficult to list other important differences between Berryman and Lowell, and these will be considered in the course of this book. But in spite of them, there is a basic and crucial similarity. In their major, great, work both poets deal with the theme of loss, and with the related theme of how order may exist in the world. Loss takes many forms and often comes to incorporate other ideas, but it is there as a constant theme. It is also there in the poems of the other middle generation poets. Schwartz's *In Dreams Begin Responsibilities* articulated loss and absence and in some respects prepares a path for the other poets to follow. Its famous title story is suffused with loss – of the parents, of relationships, of youth itself. The exploration of loss and absence continues throughout Schwartz's work. Roethke wrote some of his finest poems in *The Lost Son*, a book which in some degree prefigures *Life Studies.* Elizabeth Bishop writes of loss of the mother in 'The Village', and in her late poetry loss becomes inextricably involved with art and creativity. In *Geography III* (1976), Crusoe's isolation and deprivation provide stimuli to his imagination and creative ability. Loss runs throughout Jarrell's work, as the titles *Losses* (1948) and *The Lost World* (1965) indicate. But for him loss becomes increasingly personal rather than general or cultural. The 'losses' of the first book are the casualties of war; in the last book the 'lost world' emerges as Jarrell's own childhood.

'The art of losing isn't hard to master', writes Elizabeth Bishop in 'One Art'. The losses which the middle generation experienced do appear generic. But Berryman and Lowell came to use loss in a different way from the other poets. They came eventually to seek a poetics of loss, a form or idiom that would differ sharply from their earlier poetics. From Yeats, Tate and Ransom they had learned a poetics of recovery, of restitution. That is, the form of the poetry was totally bound up with the desire to recover past experience. But Berryman and Lowell realised that loss demanded an alternative poetics. They abandoned the possibility of a poetics of recovery: but were then faced with the need to forge a new style. They sought what Lowell called a 'rhetoric of destitution'. More than anything else, this search distinguishes Berryman and Lowell from the other middle generation poets.

Lowell's phrase occurs in a letter to Berryman. Replying to Berryman's published analysis of 'Skunk Hour', he explained why he has chosen the line 'I hear my ill spirit sob in each blood cell':

> The 'sob in each blood-cell' [sic] is meant to have a haggard, romantic profilish exaggerated quality – true, but in the rhetoric of destitution, here the mere matter of fact descriptive style gives out, won't do, and there's only the stagey for the despair.[33]

Lowell sees that some styles 'give out', and this insight forms the basis for the changes in his poetry and in Berryman's. A style 'gives out' because it belongs to another poet, or because it is unsuited to the poem's subject. Contrasted with the other poets of their generation, the styles of Berryman and Lowell changed enormously, and they are distinct from the others because they explored what remains when a particular style 'gives out'. What they finally explore are different rhetorics of destitution.

1

Beginning in Wisdom

Beginning in wisdom, dying in doubt.

('Tenth Muse')

In 1940 Berryman, aged 26, published twenty poems in the collection *Five Young American Poets*, the same book which introduced the poetry of Randall Jarrell. Most of Berryman's poems were reprinted in his first book-length collection, *Poems* (1942). Lowell too reprinted most of his first book, *Land of Unlikeness* (1944), in his second, *Lord Weary's Castle* (1946). As one begins to compare the early poetry of Berryman and Lowell a major difficulty arises. *Lord Weary's Castle* is an immense achievement. It was widely reviewed, received high praise and won the Pulitzer prize for Lowell in 1947. With this single book he quickly attained the status of a major poet. On the other hand, Berryman's *Poems* won no comparable accolade. Joel Conarroe rightly makes the point that if it were not for Berryman's later achievement, earlier work such as *Poems* would remain largely unread.[1] Much the same could be said of Roethke's first book, *Open House* (1941), although Roethke exhibits greater potential than Berryman for growth of talent. The reception given to *Lord Weary's Castle* was as great as that which had been given to Schwartz's *In Dreams Begin Responsibilities*. However, by 1944 such acclaim was beginning to turn against Schwartz. From the first Lowell seemed greater than the other poets of his generation; *Lord Weary's Castle* showed major talent that had the potential to become great.

In spite of this immediate difficulty of comparing the early work of Berryman and Lowell, there are several reasons for the validity of such a comparison. Along with Roethke and Schwartz, Berryman and Lowell are very much poets of their time, possessing a variety of stylistic similarities. Their poetry tends to be highly formal in diction and tone. They use ambiguity and irony to communicate a complex attitude to the world. Such features are of course quite typical of many poets writing during the 1940s. Like all of the middle

15

generation poets, Berryman and Lowell learnt from the New Critics and the modernists. 'He said', Lowell once wrote of Allen Tate, 'that a good poem . . . was a piece of craftsmanship, an intelligible or *cognitive* object.'[2] The New Criticism was an atmosphere fostering a particular poetic style, and both Berryman and Lowell placed their work firmly within that style.

Both began as very much poets of their time. However, Berryman's early poetry seems dated in a way that Lowell's does not. Both chose particular models for their work, as well as being influenced more generally by the New Critical atmosphere. The influence of Yeats on Berryman was really rather crushing. In his own exaggerated way Berryman tended to dismiss much of his earlier work, suggesting that his desire to *'be'* Yeats was unfortunate and overwhelming.[3] His work does seem dated, ironically for such a devoted follower of Yeats. In part, Lowell's first achievement was engendered by his potential for assimilating influences in a way that Berryman could not. Lowell absorbs atmosphere, advice and influence. But he was also able to make these interact with his own vision and talent. On re-reading *Lord Weary's Castle* Lowell once said that it seemed to be 'studded with Eliot'.[4] And yet, this is not the overall impression that the reader receives. There are echoes, many echoes. One can hear Hopkins, Tate, Ransom, Crashaw, T. S. Eliot, and can discern a broader influence from the prose of Emerson, Thoreau and Melville. But for the most part these are echoes, and Lowell uses them in highly deliberate and skilful ways. For example, part VI of 'The Quaker Graveyard in Nantucket' clearly alludes to part IV of 'The Dry Salvages'. At this point in *Four Quartets* Eliot prays to the Virgin Mary for the safety of seafarers. The prayer falls into three parts; first, on behalf of 'all those in ships', then for the relatives of those at sea, and finally for those

> . . . who were in ships, and
> Ended their voyage on the sand, in the sea's lips
> Or in the dark throat which will not reject them
> Or wherever cannot reach them the sound of the sea-bell's
> Perpetual angelus.

Lowell, though, imagines his sailor after death and emphasises our lack of knowledge about God. Rather than relying on the mercy of the Virgin he suggests her possible indifference:

Our Lady, too small for her canopy,
Sits near the altar. There's no comeliness
At all or charm in that expressionless
Face with its heavy eyelids. As before,
This face, for centuries a memory,
Non est species, neque decor,
Expressionless, expresses God: it goes
Past castled Sion. She knows what God knows . . .

The point need not be laboured. Lowell clearly uses Eliot's poem in a special way, using the echo to enrich the special quality of his own poem. He turns from the conventional prayer to the possibility of the unknowable God, whose mercy is not assured and for whom the sea may be an instrument of punishment. Lowell seems to absorb the meaning and intention of Eliot's poem, but then deflects these. His own poem becomes richer because of this strategy. Eliot's influence does not crush him; he is not here 'influenced' in the way that Berryman was 'influenced' by Yeats. Lowell shows how particular effects can be gained through intertextuality. When Berryman reminds us of Yeats we might think only that he is trying to write like Yeats. When Lowell reminds us of Eliot or Tate or Hopkins he is usually leading us to a rich and alternative vein. This quality helps to account for the enduring reputation of *Lord Weary's Castle*, contrasting with the status of Berryman's early poetry. In *Open House*, and, indeed, throughout his career, Roethke used a strategy similar to that of Lowell's in *Lord Weary's Castle*. This is largely how Roethke has challenged conventional views of poetic influence. Like Lowell, Roethke shapes and distorts poetic forbears. 'I take this cadence from a man named Yeats; / I take it and give it back again' ('Four for Sir John Davies'). The major difference is that Lowell was dissatisfied with this strategy after a time. Where Roethke continued with it, Lowell broke sharply away from poetic influence.

It is rather too easy to keep on comparing the early poetry of Berryman and Lowell to the disadvantage of Berryman. A look at their similarities should be more rewarding. As already mentioned, both are poets of the 1940s; both influenced by those whom Harold Bloom might consider their 'strong' precursors, but that influence works differently for both poets.

There is one apparently insurmountable difference between the early work of Lowell and Berryman, but some analysis of it leads to an understanding of their strong basic similarities. A major theme of Lowell's work during the 1940s is the relationship between God and humanity. While his ideas concerning this relationship owe a lot to Ransom and Tate, they do give his work an immense driving force. The very titles, 'Land of Unlikeness' and 'Lord Weary's Castle', indicate this large theme, for with them Lowell intends a description of the modern world. The 'land of unlikeness' is a phrase used by Etienne Gilson for St Augustine's 'regio dissimilitudinis'. It suggests the world of those without a sense of God.[5] In his review of *Lord Weary's Castle* Berryman himself noted the title's significance: Lowell uses the doomed 'house of ingratitude, failure of obligation, crime and punishment' to suggest our world.[6] Lowell had become a convert to Roman Catholicism in 1940. Faith gave more than theme and attitude to his poetry of the 1940s; form itself becomes an expression of his faith, of his sense of the relationship between God and humanity. Berryman, however, lacks such religious vision. True, the idea of faith appears at different moments, and is sustained as a theme in 'The Disciple', but although Berryman had been baptised and brought up as a Roman Catholic, he lost his faith during adolescence. In the 1940s he is in no sense a religious poet. He neither possesses a religious world view nor does he seek one. Even in 'The Disciple' he does not explore faith or doubt thematically. In fact, the ambiguities of this poem are rather confusing; Ian Hamilton considered Berryman to be 'floundering' in his inability to affirm faith or explore doubt.[7] Although this difference appears to be considerable, there is a comparable impulse underlying their poetry. Berryman's trust in art is derived from a source similar to that which leads to Lowell's religious poetry. Both are responses to a particular set of ideas, and both are indicative of specific attitudes to experience.

An analysis of these attitudes can begin with the ideas of Ransom and Tate, in the light of the influence that these figures exerted on the middle generation. One might here recall the advice Tate gave to Lowell about the poem as 'cognitive object', the result of 'craft'. The advice may appear straightforward. But for Tate and Ransom this idea of the poem as cognitive object summarises a range of political and religious ideas. When Lowell agrees with Tate on the nature of the poem he is in a large measure accepting that set of political and religious ideas. The very form of the early poetry of Berryman and Lowell is, for Ransom and Tate, inextricable from those ideas.

The views on poetry that Ransom and Tate held by the late 1930s were refined from ideas developed since 1920. Both men had been key members of the Fugitives, a group of Southern writers based in Nashville, Tennessee. *The Fugitive*, their magazine, existed primarily to publish the poetry of group members. It had a secondary purpose, that of examining on occasion the state of current poetry and poetics. Despite the ending of the Fugitives, a subsequent group was formed in 1930. This group, the Agrarians, was strongly regional and strongly political. Again, Ransom and Tate were key members. In fact, the Agrarians ought to be termed a movement rather than a group, since they did have particular aims, and the beliefs which they fostered were far from being exclusively literary or artistic. The collection of essays which publicly founded the movement, *I'll Take My Stand* (1930) dealt also with history, religion, politics and economics. The concerns which Ransom and Tate explored while Agrarians had a powerful impact on all of their subsequent writings on aesthetics.

To them, Agrarianism was neither metaphor or myth. It seems there are always available myths of a golden pre-industrial age. But the Agrarians believed firmly in the actual virtues of the *ante-bellum* South. What is more, they publicly agitated for the return of such virtues. Basically, the Agrarian belief was in an organic, pre-industrial order: the community close to the land, its members having the relations that existed before industrialism, and dependent ultimately on the land. Ransom, Tate and the Agrarians were not alone in such an ideal. For T. S. Eliot the excellence of tradition represented order and stability: but in a metaphorical sense. F. R. Leavis believed in the former existence of an organic, traditional community: but he also considered it as lost and unavailable to recovery.[8] The Agrarians, however, believed in the truth and the efficacy of the traditional community; and with the apparent failure of industrialism during the Depression, a return to subsistence farming appeared to them as both practical and desirable. Ransom left the teaching of literature for a year to study economic theory. By 1932 he was seriously extolling the advantages offered by a return to pre-industrialism:

It is tempting to write like a poet, philosopher or humanist about the aesthetic and spiritual deliverance that will come when the industrial laborers with their specialized and routine jobs and the business men with their offices and abstract preoccupations become translated into people handling the soil with their fingers and coming into direct contact with nature.[9]

In short, Agrarianism was not merely an imaginative theoretical postulate offered by Ransom and Tate. To them it was a serious and considered political position; and from this position they advanced a poetic theory. To them, this poetics was quite inseparable from the theoretical and political concerns underlying it. Essentially, their aesthetic theories have three main divisions: the idea of poetry as 'whole knowledge', the idea of poetry as systematic memory, and the belief in a highly formal and difficult poetry. Each of these strongly influenced the early work of the middle generation poets, and each has a firm political basis.

The concept that literature is 'whole knowledge' is central to the New Critical theory of Ransom and Tate. Of course it has its roots in nineteenth-century Romantic thought, particularly in the ideas of Coleridge. But to Ransom and Tate it was also a political, religious and specifically anti-scientific concept. Beginning from the familiar idea that industrialism intensifies the division of labour and skills in a society, they argued that an agrarian society fostered in each person a variety of skills. That is, the industrial community divided what had been united in the traditional organic community: usefulness and beauty, knowledge and sensitive appreciation, work and play. In Ransom's 1934 essay 'Poets Without Laurels' one can clearly see the transition from such a broad view of society and history to a particular aesthetic. The poem too combines usefulness and uselessness: that is, knowledge and beauty. In this sense it is 'whole knowledge' – larger and greater than reductive scientific thought, since it fuses objective precision with sensibility.

The idea that poetry represents a fusion of experience, that is whole knowledge, was explored by Tate again and again in his essays. The idea is there with special strength in 'Tension in Poetry' (1938) and in 'Literature as Knowledge' (1941). These essays have generally been considered only in terms of Tate's aesthetic theory, but this theory is in fact inseparable from his social and political theory. The essays continue with the association Ransom saw between the agrarian community and the poem, but Tate's emphasis on Agrarianism is much more subdued. He has refined his ideas from a much larger range of beliefs. In a 1930 essay 'Religion and the Old South', Tate had praised the religious attitude to experience because it transcended a scientific approach. The substance of his argument will appear again, after the end of Agrarianism: but then 'religion' will be replaced by 'poetry':

> Religion, when it directs its attention to the horse cropping the blue grass on the lawn, is concerned with the whole horse . . . The modern mind sees only half the horse – that half which may become a dynamo, or an automobile, or any other horse-powered machine.[10]

It is crucial here to note the intimate connection between the aesthetics of Ransom and Tate and a larger set of beliefs and attitudes. Berryman and Lowell at first write poetry of the sort recommended by Ransom and Tate. In doing so, that poetry is informed by a comparable range of attitudes. Eventually they break from that kind of poetry, since the large range of attitudes is no longer tenable for them. That those poetics themselves result from a series of pre-established attitudes and beliefs is often neglected. Poetry seen as whole knowledge is an example of aesthetics being derived from and supported by certain religious, political, social, historical and anti-scientific arguments. Much the same is true of the other chief aesthetic concerns of Ransom and Tate: poetry as memory and poetry as craft.

The concept of poetry as memory, as recovery, appealed quite naturally to Ransom and Tate since they believed in the need to recover and revive the *ante-bellum* Southern community. The idea recurs frequently, particularly in the work of Ransom. There it emerges as a feature of conservative ideology and part of the familiar attack on partial and reductive scientific thought:

> We live in a world which must be distinguished from the world, or the worlds . . . which we treat in our scientific discourses. They are its reduced, emasculated, and docile versions. Poetry intends to recover the denser and more refractory original world which we know loosely through our perceptions and memories.[11]

Poetry removes its subject from the realm in which it may be reduced, or in which it may become merely useful. It recovers the 'world's body' – restores to objects the full apprehension which scientific thought negates. To create poetry is to indulge in restorative action. But whereas Ransom and Tate specifically propose that poetry recovers objects and experience from science, they also imply that it redeems them from time. The poetic act is thus both recovery and preservation.

Of course, the concept of art as preservation is by no means new, nor is it exclusive in our century to Ransom and Tate. Indeed, it was shared among the New Critics: I. A. Richards called the arts 'our storehouse of recorded values'.[12] In their earlier work Berryman and Lowell become deeply committed to poetry as recovery. To them it represents an answer to the problem of loss and change, represents the capacity to freeze and escape from time. Again, Ransom and Tate had founded an aesthetic on their arguments against science and industrialism, and this aesthetic exerts a profound influence on Berryman and Lowell.

In terms of his own work and the kind of poetry he has encouraged, Tate has been associated with a difficult, formal style. His belief in this style developed most while he was associated with the Agrarians, and as such it results directly from his attacks on behaviourism. In 'Understanding Modern Poetry' (1940), he quoted some advice given to teachers of poetry:

> Comprehending a poem need not involve any intellectual or formal concern with its technique, prose content, type, moral, diction, analysis, social implications, etc. Comprehending a poem is essentially an organic experience, essentially a response to the poetic stimulus of the author.[13]

Tate is horrified and enraged by such a blatant application of the stimulus-response model to the act of reading. Poetry, he urges, is an exception to this model, because of the demands that it makes upon the individual intellect:

> When you are making a response, you are not doing anything more than a chimpanzee or a Yahoo would be doing. But should you more than respond, you might perform an act of intelligence, of knowing, of cognition. In the conditioning theory there is no cognition because there is no intelligence.[14]

From his Agrarian attacks on science, industrialism and behaviourism, Tate comes to the conclusion that good poetry must be demanding, and must eliminate the possibility of simple affective response. Ransom shared this view, reminding us that 'poetry is an artifice, practised with an adult cunning'.[15] Thus Tate's advice to Lowell, telling him that poetry is a 'cognitive object', is loaded with implications. The idea of poetry as craft derives logically from this position: the metrics of poetry distinguishing it from other forms of discourse also forbid simple affective response. But importantly, in 1935 Tate had noted that a formalist poetics could have wider implications: 'It is probable that there is an intimate relation between a generally accepted "picture of the world" and the general acceptance of a metrical system and its differentiation into patterns.'[16] Berryman, Lowell and Roethke at first accepted such a metrical system, that formal poetry proposed by Tate. In doing so, they subscribed in some measure to the accompanying 'picture of the world' that Tate and Ransom had also presented.

As an attempt at practical economics, Agrarianism ended in the late 1930s, but the theoretical ideas it had fostered remained firmly embedded in the critical ideas of Ransom and Tate. Lowell's close involvement with these figures began just as Agrarianism was being incorporated into New Critical theory. Their influence was exerted at this time also upon Roethke, Jarrell and Schwartz. Jarrell followed Ransom from Nashville to his new appointment at Kenyon in 1940, and even lived with Lowell in Ransom's house. Schwartz held a deep and prolonged respect for Ransom, and taught at the Kenyon summer school. Tate's advice to Lowell must ultimately be seen as more than just a useful hint from one poet to another. It has to be considered in the terms of its origins and implications. Its origins are in a matrix of political and religious assumptions that concern knowledge, science and experience; its implications are for a particular view of the world.

The influence of Ransom's thought on Lowell has continually been underestimated, even though the fact of their personal closeness has been noted again and again. For all of Ransom's reputation as a New Critic (he himself coined the term 'New Criticism' in his book of that title in 1941), his ideas on poetics and the ontology of poetry had mostly been developed as part of an investigation into the relationship between God and the world, and as part of his rationale of Agrarian politics. His sustained treatment of the relationship between God and humanity is in his 1930 book *God Without Thunder*.

Ransom begins the book's argument from the Kantian premise that the world is essentially unknowable. However, instead of constructing a series of propositions, like Kant, by which the world may be apprehended, Ransom's main concern is to reassert this Kantian premise in an attack on scientific thought. He argues that though science is a natural human activity, it is necessarily reductive and partial in how it represents the world's complexities:

> All the sciences . . . have their practical objectives. . . . They aim of course at reducing natural phenomena to human understanding, and to that extent they may seem disinterested and innocent. But they also aim . . . at reducing them to human prediction and control.[17]

Ransom asserts that this is impossible, the world being altogether beyond human prediction and control.

At this point Ransom argues for the significance of myth as a means of knowing the world while at the same time recognising that it cannot be known. Religion's importance to humanity lies in the fact that it is a series of ritualised myths: 'Religion is an order of experience under which we indulge the compound attitude of fear, respect, enjoyment, and love for . . . external nature. . . .'[18] Ransom goes on to examine contemporary attitudes towards God. He argues that contemporary thought is dominated by scientific rationality, which refuses to recognise the unknowable and attributes evil only to lack of knowledge. Thus the contemporary image of God is of a benign and merciful being; the 'God without thunder'. This view directly contradicts the Old Testament view of God, in which God was considered both inscrutable and potentially malevolent. Finally, Ransom pleads for a fuller 'non-scientific' view of God, and his final exhortation is in his hope that 'modern man' will 'restore to God the thunder'.[19]

There is much in *God Without Thunder* that is exaggerated and contentious; Ransom himself called it 'theological homebrew' and tended later to dismiss it.[20] But the book's influence on Lowell was considerable, and goes some way towards explaining the emphasis in *Lord Weary's Castle* on damnation, violent apocalypse, personal guilt and worldly sinfulness. As most critics have argued, Lowell combines Roman Catholicism and Calvinism in a highly individual way. We rarely feel the grace of God working benevolently or mercifully:

> Christ walks on the black water. In Black Mud
> Darts the Kingfisher. On Corpus Christi, heart,

Over the drum-beat of St Stephen's choir
I hear him, *Stupor Mundi*, and the mud –
Flies from his hunching wings and beak – my heart,
The blue kingfisher dives on you in fire.

Here the reception of grace, from 'Colloquy in Black Rock', is extremely violent rather than peaceful or tranquil. Lowell comes much closer to the frenzy of an Edwards convert than he does to the tranquillity of sacramental reception. A similar attitude is present in 'In Memory of Arthur Winslow':

O Mother, I implore
Your scorched, blue thunderbreasts of love to pour
Buckets of blessings on my burning head
Until I rise like Lazarus from the dead:
Lavabis nos et super nivem delababor

Critics have seen how ungainly and absurd the metaphor here is: more relevantly, though, one should emphasise how Lowell sees the reception of grace as physically overwhelming. Nowhere in *Lord Weary's Castle* does one receive a sense of the grace and blessings of God working silently or constantly in the world. There is also a kind of desperate glee in Lowell's view of the world's forthcoming destruction:

The flies, the flies, the flies of Babylon
Buzz in my eardrums while the devil's long
Dirge of the purple detonates the hour
For floating cities where his golden tongue
Enchants the masons of the Babel Tower
To raise tomorrow's city to the sun
That never sets upon these hell-fire streets
Of Boston, where the sunlight is a sword
Striking at the witholder of the Lord:
Flies, flies are on the plane tree, on the streets.

While Lowell's religious beliefs are personal and perhaps outside the concerns of literary criticism, they inform his poetry to a degree that invites their evaluation. The anger and despair of the poems in *Lord Weary's Castle* suggest that he has taken to heart Ransom's plea for a God with 'thunder'. Lowell thus revives the Old Testament view of God as unknowable and perhaps destructive. Strong associations exist between *God Without Thunder* and *Lord Weary's Castle*. This fact suggests a further analogy between the two books. For Lowell, as for Ransom, religion has become important primarily as the means of providing a sense of order and direction in the unknowable world, and as a means of judging reality. Of course, I am not here presuming to question the sincerity of Lowell's personal beliefs, but am assessing the poetry and its implications. In *Lord Weary's Castle* there is a powerfully expressed sense of disgust with the world. While the religious perspective may appear to be a means of dealing with the world, it is also a means of judging and eventually dismissing it. *Lord Weary's Castle* and *God Without Thunder* arise from a similar concept: there is a need for a teleological system through which the world may be known. However, it is an ambiguous system, because it incorporates within itself the belief that the world is finally unknowable. Religion is the teleological system chosen. And this is the point at which Berryman and Lowell became comparable, in spite of Berryman's lack of a specifically religious view of the world. In his early work Berryman shares Lowell's disgust with the world, and, more importantly, an inability to accept temporal mortality itself. But instead of presenting a religious attitude through which he may seek to transcend human mortality, Berryman places his trust in art. Art is the impersonal system which transcends time. It answers a need in Berryman that in Lowell is answered in religious faith. Both men affirm a larger reality. Perhaps also behind Berryman's faith in art and Lowell's religious faith lies a concept which is to surface in the later work of both writers. Lowell's faith springs from a fear of loss and disorder. Underlying Berryman's early work there is often an ill-concealed comparable fear. In 'Winter Landscape' Berryman acclaims art's timeless quality, but this attitude scarcely hides his deeper fear of time and change. The fear is made tolerable only through his belief that time may be transcended, that there exists a permanent order sealed off from time. Eventually for Berryman this belief in a permanent transcendent order diminished, and as it did so he chose in his poetry to come to terms with time and loss, to face them rather than seek to escape from them. Lowell too went through a crisis as his faith lost the strength evident in *Lord Weary's Castle*. He emerged with *Life Studies*, where the central concern is with the individual's need to accept mortality and mutability. In their early work Berryman and Lowell present art and religion as somehow equivalent to modernist myth, means of ordering 'fragments against the ruins'. In their later work they are both moved to explore those ruins, to rearrange, create afresh and even 'de-create' those fragments.

'Winter Landscape' is undoubtedly one of Berryman's finest early poems, and in it one can see clearly his concern with the need for art to transcend time. In a 1965 essay Berryman wrote that with 'Winter Landscape' he felt that he had gained an individual poetic voice. While this claim is open to dispute, there is certainly one feature of the poem which distinguishes it from his other poems of this period. As with those other poems, the influences working on Berryman may be seen. But here he uses those influences in a highly creative way. They do not crush him and they do not overwhelm the poem; he shows that he is able to subordinate them so that they come to enrich his own poem. Keats's great 'Ode on a Grecian Urn' is an unmistakable precursor, and Yeats (who else?) also provides a strong source for the poem.

But Berryman absorbs these poems and ideas, making them conform to his own perspective. It is true that at times he seems to come rather too close to Keats: one cannot miss the similarity of movement and gesture between the two poems. Keats extols the urn's transcendence of time: 'When old age shall this generation waste, / Thou shalt remain . . .'. Berryman uses similar phraseology to communicate much the same idea: 'when all their company / will have been irrevocably lost', the picture will communicate 'What place, what time, what morning occasion / / sent them into the woods.' In this respect, though, one can see a difference between Berryman and Keats, a moment at which Berryman borrows the movement and theme of Keats's poem and turns it into a movement of his own. Keats asked what the pictures on the urn represented:

> What men or gods are these? What maidens loth?
> What mad pursuit? What struggle to escape?
> What pipes and timbrels? What wild ecstasy?

Of course, these questions become central to Keats's theme, as they lead him towards the problem concerning the relationship between art and time. The urn is beyond time but Keats presents such an awareness of the problems that this condition involves that he cannot totally affirm such immutability. He suggests that the urn's removal from the flux of time also removes it from the human sphere. The human and natural actions that the urn depicts frozenly become almost nonsensical in terms of immutability, since their status as actions implies commitment to temporal progression:

> Bold Lover, never, never canst thou kiss,
> Though winning near the goal – yet, do not grieve;
> She cannot fade, though thou has not thy bliss,
> For ever wilt thou love, and she be fair!
>
> Ah, happy, happy, boughs! that cannot shed
> Your leaves, nor ever bid the Spring adieu;

The point here is that Keats's poem involves a paradox concerning the relationship between art and reality, timelessness and change. In 'Sailing to Byzantium' Yeats had also explored the paradoxical relationship between art and time. Having desired to escape from time Yeats introduces the singing golden bird as a symbol of timeless, immutable art. But when the bird sings it must sing of things and events which belong properly to time; of 'What is past, or passing, or to come.' The singing itself relies upon time. On the urn, nature and humanity were represented in a way that denied their commitment to time and made them seem almost ridiculous. Yeats's 'golden bird' has to return to the dimension of time to sing meaningfully to us.

These points have been made by other critics and require little further analysis here. But the awareness of Keats and Yeats, that the supposedly unalterable, immutable status of the art-work is complex and even ambiguous, is not here shared by Berryman. In using Keats's poem the way he does Berryman acknowledges his awareness of the potentially ambiguous relationship. But he affirms almost unequivocally the permanent order which art provides. Berryman might be correct in his assertion that with 'Winter Landscape' he achieved his individual voice, in that he uses the precursor poems to add strength to his own poem; they do not overwhelm him, crush him with their power.

'Winter Landscape', then, is a celebration of art itself. It explores no paradox, and is rather dismissive of the world beyond the picture: Berryman writes rather rhetorically of the 'evil waste of history' from which the picture is redeemed. In fact, the whole idea of art being somehow redeemed from time and chaos links Berryman very closely with the attitudes of Ransom, Tate and

Lowell. Ransom in particular had argued at length that art itself is a redemptive action resulting from a human instinct to preserve from the flux of time. He had associated religion and art very closely in this respect – and, as mentioned above, this link between art and religion helps us to consider Berryman and Lowell as much closer than has been hitherto suggested. Lowell seeks to transcend contemporary reality through affirming a religious view, while Berryman presents art transcending time. In 'Winter Landscape' this idea of transcendence of time is in part expressed technically through the use which Berryman makes of time shifts. The poem begins in the present tense, although Berryman holds back the main verb until the opening of line eleven. The present participles of the first two stanzas are given special emphasis, particularly 'returning', made notably prominent as the first word of the fifth and sixth lines. Similarly, the first main verb is conspicuously placed. Thus Berryman begins with an emphasis on how the action of the picture must be apprehended as though it were taking place now. It is almost paradoxical, then, that to the men history belongs in the future; and Berryman makes clever use of this paradox:

> . . . in the sandy time
> To come, the evil waste of history
> Outstretched, they will be seen upon the brow
> Of that same hill: when all their company
> Will have been irrevocably lost . . .

Their transcendence of time and history is presented powerfully through this use of tense. The men will be seen as they are now, but by the eyes of the future. Their fellows cannot be redeemed from time; and Berryman's use of the future perfect, usually a clumsy tense, is here exactly appropriate. Briefly, the poem uses the past tense, but only in a subordinate clause. The phrase in which this past tense is used serves a special purpose for Berryman, providing as it does an echo of 'Ode on a Grecian Urn'; the men

> . . . will keep the scene and say
> By their configuration with the trees,
> The small bridge, the red houses and the fire,
> What place, what time, what morning occasion
> Sent them into the wood . . .

The subordinate clause in the past tense is succeeded by a return to the present tense and a main verb. From the woods the men return 'as we now see them'. There are some clear implications of this use of the main tense. Now it is we, as observers of the picture and thus of the scene, who are in the present tense. At this moment in the poem their transcendence of time through the medium of art is enacted and made complete. They are present to the observers of the picture, and always will be to different observers at different times. Through art they have become part of a continual present, saved from time. Berryman affirms this idea still more with 'flies', the poem's final word also a verb in the present tense. The movement of the poem involves or enacts a chronological shift, but during it the hunters remain in the present. This use of different tenses reinforces the idea of art as a continual present, a means of escaping time's destructive progression. Robert Graves made much the same point in considering Caliban's celebrated speech which begins 'Be not afeard. The isle is full of noises' (*The Tempest*, iii, ii). Graves argued that Caliban's apparent confusion of tenses creates a dramatically important 'suspension' of time.[21] While Keats and Yeats explore the paradox involved in art's apparent defeat of time, Berryman avoids the paradox so that he may celebrate art's timeless order, its permanently present tense.

'Winter Landscape', then, is a poem about art, in which art attains the status of myth. It tells of a supposedly permanent truth, art transcending the temporal flux, escaping the 'evil waste of history'. Such a view of art emerges in several different poems by Berryman written around this time. In 'The Statue' he uses a statue to symbolise the permanence of art – a use analogous to the way in which Stevens presents the statue of General Du Puy in 'Notes Towards A Supreme Fiction'. However, for Stevens the statue's immutability renders it valueless: 'yet the general was rubbish in the end'. For Berryman, though, the permanence of the statue serves to accentuate the time-bound transient lives of those who live near it:

> The lovers pass. Not one of them can know
> Or care which Humboldt is immortalized.
> If they glance up, they glance in passing,
> An idle outcome of that pacing
> That never stops, and proves them animal;
> These thighs breasts pointed eyes are not their choosing,

But blind insignia by which are known
Season, excitement, loosed upon this city.

In emphasising the time-bound existence of the people, Berryman
tends to be impatiently dismissive of them. It is an attitude shared
by Lowell in *Lord Weary's Castle*. The association is interesting partly
because both writers come eventually to a point at which they can
accept and even embrace humanity's time-bound status. 'The
Statue' ends with an image of future suicide. An 'insignificant
dreamer'

> . . . will close his eyes
> Mercifully on the expensive drama
> Wherein he wasted so much skill, such faith,
> And salvaged less than the intolerable statue.

Seeking escape, the suicide may consider death a 'merciful' release
from time. While alive, his failure seems to be felt through his
inevitable commitment to time itself, his inability to defeat it. The
statue has become intolerable to him primarily because it stands
outside of the flux of time, thus mocking his own mortality. Since he
is an 'occupant' of time, 'defeated' by it, he is unable to achieve
comparable transcendence. In fact in this poem there is an implied
idea that the suicide's action is a kind of work of art, an action in
which his 'skill' would not be wasted, and an act of salvage or
redemption, born out of both desire and despair. In these early
poems the ideas are much deeper than a simple 'ars longa vita brevis'.
Berryman places a religious trust in art as transcendent, redemptive;
he does not see it merely as something outlasting time.

I am trying here to see beyond the religious attitudes of Lowell's
poetry, trying to show how he and Berryman display a finally
comparable range of attitudes in their early work. In the poems just
considered, Berryman uses a painting and a statue to symbolise art's
capacity to defeat the flux of time. Lowell uses symbolism in a very
similar way, and to a similar end, although in his work time is
supposedly defeated by permanent and universal faith. The
symbolist technique is central to the early poetry of Berryman and
Lowell, and their use of it is a strong indicator of their similarities. I
want here to return to the ideas of Ransom and Tate; not only
because of their particular influence on Lowell or because they

created an atmosphere which involved particular attitudes to poetry, but mainly because their general concern with the symbol highlights the overall techniques and themes of Lowell and Berryman.

As we have seen, Ransom and Tate believed that poetry is essentially recovery. It was also a restoration of the complexity of experience – a complexity under threat from reductive scientific approaches. Because of this attitude to poetry, the symbol became for Ransom and Tate the essential distinguishing feature of poetic discourse. The symbol represented whole knowledge because it contained, held, ambiguities; because it conveyed the complexity of experience; and because it combined skill with beauty. In their most renowned essays on poetry Ransom and Tate often concluded with an affirmation of the symbolist technique.

A major reason behind the use of symbolism in *Lord Weary's Castle* is Lowell's need to convey ambiguity, rejecting a simplistic view of experience. Such a use of symbol can clearly be seen in 'The Holy Innocents'. The poem is a symbolic dramatisation of the ambiguities of innocence, meekness and humility. The use of oxen as symbolic of Christ's followers suggests the range of this ambiguity. In the Old Testament certain oxen were raised to be pure for sacrifice. Hence the association between purity, innocence and death, by which Lowell expresses the dangerous aspect of innocence. Though innocence is a condition necessary to salvation, it is a virtue that makes its owner very vulnerable in the world. The very title 'The Holy Innocents' points to this ironical relationship between innocence and destruction. The fine qualities of the poem derive from Lowell's use of symbolic language to express the conflicts and complexities of experience. An understanding of the poem requires the recognition of how these ambiguities are rendered symbolically. This is one of the ways that Lowell uses symbolism: to achieve a concentrated discourse that can assimilate and contain contradictory aspects of experience.

However, there is another major reason behind Lowell's use of the symbol. When Ransom argues that poetry is an act of redemption, of recovery, one might quite reasonably question the basis of such recovery. From what does poetry recover 'the world's body'? From science, of course, Ransom would argue, from the rigid reductions of scientific rationality. But Ransom and Tate also imply that poetry redeems experience from the passage of time. The symbolist and imagist technique is to freeze a moment or experience within a particular image or structure, making the idea or experience somehow inaccessible or immune to time. To Ransom and Tate this was an ideal concept: the symbol, and hence the poem, could somehow enclose and protect the experience. These views were obviously common. The celebrated descriptions of the poem which originated during the most influential period of the New Criticism emphasised the poem's spatial qualities. I am thinking here of W. K. Wimsatt's 'verbal icon' and of Cleanth Brooks's appropriation of the phrase 'well-wrought urn'. The poem is considered in spatial rather than temporal terms because, after all, its distinct quality is to enclose and preserve rather than change in time.

So, when Berryman chooses symbols of timeless art he selects the statue and the painting, precisely because they are static. They are uncommitted to time and movement, unlike, say, music or dance: Berryman would undoubtedly have approved of Schelling's remark that 'architecture in general is frozen music'. Of course there is T. S. Eliot's celebrated complaint from *Four Quartets* that

> Words strain,
> Crack and sometimes break, under the burden,
> Under the tension, slip, slide, perish,
> Decay with imprecision, will not stay in place,
> Will not stay still.

In his early work Berryman attempts to defeat this problem by having his art aspire to the condition of painting or sculpture. Behind Berryman's technique and the symbols he selects is an attitude to time and loss, an attitude which is shared by Lowell. It is crucial to see that the use of the symbol is for Berryman and Lowell part of an attempt to escape the flux of time. In fact, it is tempting here to anticipate *Life Studies*. The book was important in so many respects, but one of the most striking features of its technique was Lowell's refusal to create symbolic discourse. He once called *Life Studies* a 'book without symbols', and the implications of the statement are enormous. Primarily, it suggests that Lowell no longer considers the need to escape from time and is exploring ways of living within its remorselessly linear progression.

So, ideally at least, the symbol transcends time. In *Lord Weary's Castle* Lowell has another reason for using a symbolist mode. As with Berryman, the symbol best enacts the preserving function that was considered the essence of art. But in this book Lowell goes further. He attempts to see beyond reality to a higher order that is permanent and universal. In achieving this end, the symbol represents an important poetic strategy. Essentially, it derives from the attempt to discover – or uncover – spiritual significance in the material world, to interpret the world's objects and see through them to the spiritual world beyond. We must, I think, here take into account the influence of Hopkins on Lowell. He admired Hopkins greatly, not only for his energetic use of language, but as a model of the religious poet. For Hopkins, poetry should uncover or reveal the innate order of an object, its 'inscape' or its 'instress': 'design, pattern, or what I am in the habit of calling "inscape" is what I above all aim at in poetry.'[22] The poet creates a specific order in the poem, and in doing so seeks to make manifest the essential individual nature of the subject. For Hopkins a spiritual dimension was clearly involved. The poem for him became an attempt to understand and reveal God's order as it is made manifest in individual objects. Through his poetic technique and beliefs Hopkins expresses a religious, meditative attitude towards external reality. Through meditation on the material he seeks insight into and affirmation of a higher, spiritual order. The form of the individual poem is itself an expression of belief in the spiritual order. Lowell was very receptive to the idea that the poem represents an ordering of experience and a spiritual exercise. When he reviewed *Four Quartets* in 1943 he wrote:

> My own feeling is that *union with God* is somewhere in sight in all poetry, though it is usually rudimentary and misunderstood.[23]

It is misunderstood because it exists for Lowell, as for Hopkins, not necessarily in terms of subject-matter but in the very act of ordering the poem's elements. A symbolist discourse is entirely appropriate to Lowell's religious perspective, and the form of any individual poem also has a spiritual quality for him. I believe that much the same is true of Berryman, even though he is without a specifically religious world view. The order of the poem is the order of art, itself a teleology that stands against time and disorder.

The point here is straightforward enough. Behind the brilliant craft of the early poetry of Berryman and Lowell lies a deep-rooted need for order. The formal poetics arise from this need: so too do Berryman's trust in art, and Lowell's religious vision.

2
Towards a Rhetoric of Destitution

'. . . in the rhetoric of destitution, . . . the more matter of fact style gives out, won't do, and there's only the stagey for the despair.'

(Lowell to Berryman, 1962)

With the publication of *Life Studies* in 1959, Lowell was able to identify in his work a radically different strategy which he here called the 'rhetoric of destitution'. Leaving aside for the moment the wider implications of the phrase, one thing it suggests is how Lowell realised that writing about loss required a fresh poetic. I will examine in the next chapter the particular poetic that emerges in *Life Studies*, and concentrate here on how Lowell moved towards that style during the 1950s. *The Mills of the Kavanaughs* (1951) has usually been considered a failure, and it is easy to concede the criticisms made of it. However, at the least the book is a very interesting failure, sharing as it does aspects of Lowell's later and earlier styles. It was written and published during a period when both Lowell and Berryman were producing work which we can now regard as transitional. Berryman's major work of this time was *The Dispossessed* (1948). Here he reprinted work from his preceding books and also included recent work appearing for the first time in book form. Like *The Mills of the Kavanaughs*, *The Dispossessed* seems to look backwards as well as forward. Several elements of Berryman's later poetry are introduced in this book – notably, in 'The Ball Poem' and 'The Nervous Songs'. It is no coincidence that in the same year as *The Dispossessed* was published Berryman started to work on the poem that would firmly establish his highly individual poetic style, *Homage to Mistress Bradstreet*. It is as though publication of *The Dispossessed* cleared a new space for Berryman, allowing him to view his earlier work as part of a completed period; while also introducing in the newer work suggestions of new paths he might follow.

Perhaps, though, it is only knowledge of later books that allows us to see *The Dispossessed* and *The Mills of the Kavanaughs* as transitional works. As such, we have to be careful with chronology itself. For example, although 'The Ball Poem' appears to break with the earlier poetry and clear a way for Berryman's later themes and style, it is itself quite an early poem. Berryman first published it privately in a pamphlet distributed to friends at Christmas 1942. The version published in *The Dispossessed* has only three very minor changes from the 1942 version.[1] In spite of this early date, critics have consistently seen it as a crucial poem in Berryman's development, and their views have been backed up by Berryman himself.[2] It is dangerous to establish a pattern which perverts chronology. Nevertheless 'The Ball Poem' does remain distinct from Berryman's other early work, and it well repays close attention.

The Ball Poem

What is that boy now, who has lost his ball,
What, what is he to do? I saw it go
Merrily bouncing, down the street, and then
Merrily over – there it is in the water!
No use to say 'O there are other balls':
An ultimate shaking grief fixes the boy
As he stands rigid, trembling, staring down
All his young days into the harbour where
His ball went. I would not intrude on him,
A dime, another ball, is worthless. Now
He senses first responsibility
In a world of possessions. People will take balls,
Balls will be lost always, little boy,
And no one buys a ball back. Money is external.
He is learning, well behind his desperate eyes,
The epistemology of loss, how to stand up
Knowing what every man must one day know
And most know many days, how to stand up.
And gradually light returns to the street,
A whistle blows, the ball is out of sight,
Soon part of me will explore the deep and dark
Floor of the harbour . . . I am everywhere,
I suffer and move, my mind and my heart move
With all that move me, under the water
Or whistling, I am not a little boy.

In 1965 Berryman wrote that the significance of 'The Ball Poem' was that it showed him how a particular use of pronouns could 'reserve' a 'commitment to identity'.[3] But the reader is probably struck more by the theme of the poem and how it differs from the attitudes of Berryman's other work. In 'Winter Landscape' and several other poems Berryman had affirmed art as permanent, transcending morality, rising above our human reliance on time. I suggested above that 'Winter Landscape' showed Berryman accepting the ideas of Ransom and Tate concerning poetry as recovery. 'The Ball Poem' is surprising and important because in it Berryman appears to reject these ideas. He is moving away from a need either to seek transcendence or recovery, and towards the ability to accept and explore loss. Thus, although the poem's theme is a fairly familiar one – through loss the boy is initiated into a new stage of life – it also suggests that Berryman is radically shifting his views on art's relation to experience.

Berryman's strategy in the opening lines is used to indicate how deeply the status of the boy's existence is affected by loss. The question 'What is the boy . . . to do' is interrupted by the insertion of a relative clause and by repetition. The introduction of the main verb is delayed, suggesting that Berryman is asking 'What is the boy now?' The idea of loss leading to initiation is established fairly quickly and develops very little. The boy is seen looking into his past 'staring down / All his young days into the harbour where / His ball went.' Then the process of initiation becomes more explicit. The boy is shown learning 'how to stand up / Knowing what every man must one day know / And most know many days, how to stand up.' The narrator of the poem recognises that the boy must undergo his initiation alone, without comfort or assistance. Thus on one of its levels the poem's theme is quite familiar: reaction to certain events precipitates development from one stage of growth to another.

However, initiation represents only one of the poem's aspects, and two further points need to be made even about this aspect. First of all, the boy's initiation starts because of something, an accident, which happens to him. It is not started through conscious action on his part. In this respect it differs somewhat from other patterns and stories concerning initiation – notably from one of Berryman's favourites, Faulkner's *The Bear*. Secondly, the last seven lines of the poem depart from the theme of initiation. Not altogether away from it, but far enough to qualify assumptions about what forms the poem's central theme. Berryman is using the theme of initiation to bring forward other themes, such as the universality of privation and the need to accept rather than defy time and change.

I suggested above how Berryman's early poetry usually employs a symbolist technique, the best illustrations of this being 'Winter Landscape' and 'The Statue'. But in this poem Berryman has interrupted such a symbolist discourse, by resisting the temptation to make the boy's ball into a symbol. The reader may not resist this temptation, because perhaps the most obvious interpretation is that the ball is a symbol for time, the boy's loss of the ball thus involving his initiation into the idea that lost time is irredeemable. But the poem only hints at this possibility: the ball is neither obviously nor necessarily a symbol. Given the poem's themes, this strategy is crucial. An association should be noted here between this poem and an early poem by Delmore Schwartz, 'The Ballad of the Children of the Czar'. In this poem, from Schwartz's first book, he examines the connections between himself as a very young child in 1916, eating a baked potato, and the children of Czar Nicholas II throwing a ball to each other. Eventually the ball is lost, and the baked potato falls from the baby's reach. The poem's power lies in the impressive range of implications that Schwartz explores. In particular, he examines the way that the individual is a result of the past, and is thus powerless before history. He also considers the idea that at some point in life the individual must recognise his or her inability to assert will upon the world. Thus the child Schwartz and the Czar's children are made to see their own powerlessness enacted in the losses they undergo. The ball of the children, associated throughout with the potato, is linked to the world itself: 'The ground on which the ball bounces / Is another bouncing ball.' The ball is connected also with the trust the children have in the permanence of larger things – the sun, the moon, the stars. However, their trust is dissipated since they are forced into recognising that flux is the principle on which life is based.

There are clearly some thematic connections between 'The Ball Poem' and 'The Ballad of the Children of the Czar'. But Schwartz's technique of making the ball symbolic is not used similarly by Berryman. While both poems express the need to accept the flux of time and experience, Berryman implies that a symbolic discourse is inappropriate to this view. As can be seen in Lowell's 'Beyond the Alps', a refusal to symbolise represented quite an appropriate strategy for Lowell and Berryman in poems which involve the need to accept the flux of experience. In their first work, the symbolist discourse was of immense significance. As it did for Ransom and Tate, the symbol evaded the flux of time, and in using the symbol Berryman and Lowell aimed for a permanence transcending time. But here Berryman's symbolism breaks down. 'The Ball Poem' represents a move away from modernist and New Critical ideas, both technically and thematically. Instead of resisting time Berryman allows his poetry to open up to it.

Appropriately, 'The Ball Poem' provides a strong sense of movement. I suggested that in 'Winter Landscape' and 'The Statue' Berryman represented art attempting to achieve the status of 'frozen music': painting or sculpture rather than music or dance. Yet here there is a commitment to time, to the dynamic rather than the static:

> . . . I am everywhere,
> I suffer and move, my mind and heart move
> With all that move me . . .

The poem itself provides a distinct pattern in which loss and grief are made universal and become also characteristic of maturity. Both 'The Ball Poem' and 'The Ballad of the Children of the Czar' focus on the moment when the child recognises a radical dissociation between self and world, and realises at once the world's independence of the will. Roethke was also to focus on this moment in the second section of *Praise to the End* (1951). For both Roethke and Schwartz the emphasis is on lost innocence. Schwartz's poem is tragic in its scope and tone. The powerful influences of Blake and Wordsworth that operate on *The Lost Son* and *Praise to the End* enrich the quality of Roethke's sense of despair at the loss of childhood innocence. But in 'The Ball Poem' Berryman emphasises that the boy has attained a vital knowledge, has achieved a necessary stage of growth. He implies how far the boy's loss is a positive force, and deftly insinuates the boy's capacity to find fulfilment after loss – 'And gradually light returns to the street . . .'. Also, the boy's loss is offset by his initiation into an adult community which is characterised by loss itself.

'The Ball Poem' offers several temptations to the reader aware of Berryman's development. One of these is to see it as concerned with Berryman's own initiation: his former poetic becoming lost to him and the resultant need to seek another. This would certainly seem to be an idea in Lowell's 'Beyond The Alps', but here it may seem rather far-fetched. The most elementary evidence – that provided by chronology – is against it, since Berryman did not break away so readily from his established style. Nevertheless, in spite of its early date, 'The Ball Poem' seems to offer possibilities for a new poetics, opportunities which Berryman eventually took up.

When Berryman looked back on the poem in 1965 he argued that it relied on a strategy involving pronouns: the poet is 'both left in and put out; the boy does and does not become him and we are confronted with a process which is at once a process of life and a process of art'.[4] However, the relationship between the poet and the boy is not especially problematic for the reader. Berryman rather seems to be anticipating the poet-subject relationship of *Homage to Mistress Bradstreet* and the Dream Songs. The identities of each are much more problematic in those poems, but one should at least consider seriously Berryman's assertion that he would have been unable to write his major work unless he had written 'The Ball Poem'. On the other hand, it seems surprising that Berryman did not mention the importance of 'The Nervous Songs' in the account of how his poetry changed and developed. This group of nine poems was written during 1943, and the similarities between them and the Dream Songs are quite striking; the most obvious being that they are designed as 'songs' and that each has a structure very similar to that of each Dream Song. An important difference is that each Nervous Song is sung by a different voice: they are not unified in the same way as the Dream Songs. However, they are sung by outsiders or by people who appear to be on the extremity of an event or feeling. Berryman's failure to provide a narrative context tends further to emphasise the almost dislocated perspective of each persona.

With 'The Nervous Songs' Berryman came close to the style of *Homage to Mistress Bradstreet*. While he has not yet developed an explicit relationship between poet and persona – a crucial element in the poem – or the possibilities offered by syntactical distortion, the clipped sentences and the stanzaic structure are already there, along with an obliqueness of reference:

> A fierce wind roaring high up in the bare
> Branches of trees, – I suppose it was lust
> But it was holy and awful. All day I thought
> I am a bobbing cork, irresponsible child

Loose on the waters. – What have you done at last?
A little work, a little vague chat.

('Young Woman's Song')

In the Dream Songs Henry is Berryman and is not Berryman. The Nervous Songs do not offer such a distorted relationship between Berryman and the singer of each song. Nevertheless, they are of distinct importance in Berryman's development. He was realising in part the possibilities offered through the use of a variety of personae speaking (or singing) from the borders of common experience. It was a strategy of which Lowell also was to make use in the development of his own individual style. The most striking examples of Lowell's use of dramatic monologue occur in the first and third parts of *Life Studies*. As with the Nervous Songs, Lowell chose characters from the extremity of experience, or at some crisis point. Eventually the reader is prepared for the introduction of Lowell himself as a persona in the fourth part of the book.

Generally, as a poetic device the monologue proved important to Berryman and Lowell in establishing their own individual voices. *The Mills of the Kavanaughs* comprises seven poems, every one of which is a dramatic monologue. Emphasis on the monologue continues in *Life Studies*, though there the technique is gradually discarded in favour of Lowell's own voice. Of course, the monologue has always flourished, and it was always present to some degree in the earlier work of Berryman and Lowell. But at this point in their careers the technique appears to have assumed a fresh significance for them. In the Nervous Songs and in poems such as 'The Mad Negro Soldier' it allowed them to explore alternative perspectives on experience. In this way it seems to have provided them with the opportunity of escape from their own styles, releasing new possibilities from the voices they already possessed. It would be far too glib and simplistic to argue that the monologue offered a kind of bridge between their early work and their later voices, but there is some truth in the assertion.

It is also interesting that both Berryman and Lowell should choose figures of alienation or extremity as personae. It is as though their earlier belief in a unifying art or in a unifying religion has been dissipated and has been broken down into a series of alternative perspectives. The New Critical 'whole knowledge' for which their earlier work strived is being disintegrated. Instead of the individual poem holding and balancing the conflicts of experience, integrating and transforming them into irony and ambiguity, the conflicts and contradictions themselves are now being explored. Instead of striving for unity, Berryman and Lowell are exploring what is offered by disunity, coming to concentrate on individual apprehensions of experience and history.

But not yet. *The Mills of the Kavanaughs* indicates that for Lowell the process of stylistic transition was very difficult. In his poetry up to 1946 he had developed a highly successful technique in which his Roman Catholicism and his poetics were inseparable. Since the late 1940s, however, Lowell's allegiance to the Church weakened considerably; and it effectively ended in 1948 when he and Jean Stafford were divorced. In 1949 he married Elizabeth Hardwick.

These events indicate a radical shift in Lowell's ideas, and this shift had serious and far-reaching consequences for his poetry. In *Lord Weary's Castle* theme and technique are inseparable. The problem which loss of belief presented for Lowell was thus technical as well as thematic. *The Mills of the Kavanaughs* was published in 1951. The book is a dense, difficult and obscure work: it was viewed by several contemporary critics as a sad, though perhaps momentary, decline in Lowell's talent. Coming as it does between *Lord Weary's Castle* and *Life Studies* it shares interesting features of both books while remaining a failure compared to the high standards set by them.

The book's title poem is preceded by two quotations which are of special significance:

> Ah, love let us be true
> To one another! For the world, which seems
> To lie before us like a land of dreams . . .

> Morals are the memory of success
> that no longer succeeds.

Both Arnold and William Carlos Williams are here concerned with the breakdown of shared, established ways of perceiving the world and acting in it. Lowell's choice of this moment from 'Dover Beach' was perhaps intended to indicate an acceptance of faith's diminution and acceptance of a world without faith being made possible by the consolation of personal relationships. Although

Arnold's poem is far from optimistic, ending as it does with the 'clash' of 'ignorant armies', Lowell has chosen the poem's most affirmative moment. However, 'The Mills of the Kavanaughs' is a very bleak poem, which itself provides little sense of salvation or consolation. The epigraph from Williams' *In The American Grain* suggests an end to forms and the necessity of moving on.[5] Perhaps Lowell found in this epigraph some personal consolation for his denial of Roman Catholicism. But if, as Williams also put it, 'divorce is a sign of knowledge in our time', there is a lack of evidence in 'The Mills of the Kavanaughs' to support so positive a view.

Although some of the ideas suggested by these epigraphs become significant in Lowell's later work, they really bear very little relevance to 'The Mills of the Kavanaughs'. The poem is mostly narrated by Anne Kavanaugh, a great deal of it being monologue. She looks back over her life and her marriage, and seems to reach some kind of resolution giving her the capacity to accept death. A great deal of the poem concentrates on the decline and breakdown of her marriage to Harry Kavanaugh. The Kavanaughs are a Catholic family, but the ending of the marriage becomes analogous to the decline and end of religious belief. Harry undergoes mental disturbances before killing himself. Anne considers the meaning of these experiences and the poem ends as she rows out on to the lake. It seems that she is about to commit suicide; whether this is so or not, she certainly appears to have achieved a readiness to accept her own death.

This brief account of the long poem is deliberately simple. The story itself is made extremely complex and dense through Lowell's sustained use of mythical allusion and association, present from the very first stanza:

> . . . There's a sort of path
> Or rut of weeds that serpents down a hill
> And graveyard to a ruined burlap mill;
> There, a maternal nineteenth century
> Italian statue of Persephone
> Still beckons to a mob of Bacchanals.

Lowell's use of a mythic framework, ostensibly that of Persephone and Pluto, tends to make the narrative very confusing, and it also considerably weakens the potential force of Lowell's

characterisation. The marriage becomes for Anne a kind of enforced
descent into hell, an idea that is made quite explicit as early on as the
third stanza:

> . . . once I bent
> Above your well, where lawn and battlement
> Were trembling, yet without a flaw to mar
> Their sweet surrender. Ripples seemed to star
> My face, the rocks, the bottom of the well;
> My heart, pursued by all its plunder, fell,
> And I was tossing petals from my lair
> Of copper leaves above your mother's chair.

This is her fall, but too many questions remain unanswered.
Basically, Lowell creates an association between Anne and
Persephone so that Anne's acceptance of death as a natural part of
life may be foregrounded and made to seem a more universal
experience. But the problem arises when Lowell worries the mythic
association, extending it until the reader is bewildered as to its
particular significance and relevance.

Hugh Staples has defended Lowell's use of myth by comparing it
to the way in which Pound, Eliot and Joyce use mythic reference.[6]
But these writers tended to use myth so that it seemed inseparable
from the poem or story, and often unobtrusively so, while allowing
myth to enrich and deepen aspects of their own work. Lowell's use
of the Persephone myth here clogs his own adopted narrative style,
and weakens rather than enriches his potentially powerful human
story. The most successful parts of 'The Mills of the Kavanaughs'
work as they are relieved of their mythic baggage and gain their own
force and momentum in its absence. The energy deriving from this
freedom may be seen in the twenty-fourth stanza. There, Anne
recalls a dream she had one Christmas morning. As she dreamt of
her husband's former vitality, Harry imagines that she dreams of
some current lover. Furiously he wakes her and demands the name
of this lover:

> I couldn't tell you; but you shook the bed,
> And struck me, Harry. 'I will shake you dead
> As earth,' you chattered, 'you, you, you, you, you . . .
> Who are you keeping, Anne?' You mocked me, 'Anne,
> You want yourself' I gagged and then I ran.

My maid was knocking. Snow was chasing through
The open window. 'Harry, I am glad
You tried to kill me; it is out, you know;
I'll shout it from the housetops of the Mills;
I'll tell you, so remember, you are mad;
I'll tell them, listen Harry: husband kills
His wife for dreaming. You must help. No, No!
I've always loved you; I am just a girl;
You mustn't choke me!' Then I thought the beams
Were falling on us. Things began to whirl.
'Harry, we're not accountable for our dreams.'

The monologue form becomes most effective here, and it is difficult
not to admire the range of effects as the narrative develops
unhampered by myth. At such points Lowell suddenly breaks
through the confusions and limitations of his mythic symbols,
achieving powerful effects relevant to the human aspect of the story.

Despite these moments of breakthrough, it is hard to consider
'The Mills of the Kavanaughs' a successful poem. Its symbols and
myths make it very dense and forbidding. The symbolisation of
experience so exactly appropriate to his earlier poetry has here
merely become a method, making the poem cluttered and obscure.
As this remains Lowell's method throughout the book, the reader
would tend to agree with Steven Axelrod's judgement that five of
the book's seven poems are 'stunning failures'.[7] Although the
poems do come close to Lowell's later attitudes and themes,
Lowell's technique fails as a means of apprehending or dealing with
aspects of experience that are fresh to his work.

The book's most obvious failures are 'David and Bathsheba in the
Public Garden' and 'Thanksgiving's Over'. The former poem is
obscure and clogged with symbols which seem to have no set
referential value: Lowell himself later called the poem 'confusing'.[8]
Lowell ignores the very human possibilities offered by the dialogue
between David and Bathsheba, and his concentration on a wider
vision of guilt and despair makes the poem too abstract, at odds
with the nature of the relationship between the lovers. In
'Thanksgiving's Over' the general impenetrability of *The Mills of the
Kavanaughs* becomes extreme. A mad suicide is recalled by her
dreaming widower, Michael. In particular, he recalls her obsession
with birds and the confusing associations she makes between them
and aspects of religious faith. One of the poem's themes appears to

be that the woman's original conception of God as being beyond the temporal world has destroyed her capacity for loving things of this world. She becomes insane because of her inability to cope with this 'land of unlikeness'. Sent to an asylum, her sense of alienation is exacerbated, and she comes to blame Michael for destroying her life instinct. She kills herself by leaping from a window.

At the end of the poem Michael prays but hears nothing in reply. As he awaits some reply the poem ends with a powerful sense of God's distance from the world. In the poem Lowell seems to place love and religion in polar opposition, thus providing a perspective on his epigraph from 'Dover Beach'. However, this opposition is by no means clear or well established, and it does not help much in interpretation of such a dense and difficult poem.

Obscurity is also apparent in 'Falling Asleep Over the Aeneid', though this poem does break through the technique that would tend to make it impenetrable. The confusions of past and present are here quite deliberate, and the fact that the old man is 'falling asleep' tends to give his associations a contextual validity. The poem suggests the need for moving through time while mantaining the importance of the past. The old man finally affirms the passing of time, the vital aspects of experience:

> Church is over, and its bell
> Frightens the yellowhammers, as I wake
> And watch the whitecaps wrinkle up the lake.

For Lowell the acceptance of the flux of time is closely involved with loss of faith, the loss of a world view in which permanence was valued. The phrase 'Church is over' and the concluding emphasis on natural flux imply an association with Wallace Stevens' great poem 'Sunday Morning'. But whereas 'Sunday Morning' ends with a celebration of the present and of the natural cycle, Lowell's poem returns to the past. In giving his bounty to the dead the old man has done what the woman in Stevens' poem refused to do. Lowell ends with a sense of the past alive in the present moment: 'It is I, I hold / His sword to keep from falling . . .'. The legacy is that of keeping the past alive rather than accepting its death, of asserting continuity in flux rather than permanence through stasis.

While 'Falling Asleep Over the Aeneid' is one of the paths Lowell takes away from *Lord Weary's Castle*, the book's most successful poem takes another. 'Mother Marie Therese' is one of Lowell's finest poems, and it anticipates *Life Studies* in its range and treatment of theme. The poem is another monologue, here narrated by a Canadian nun recalling her former Mother Superior, named in the title. Mother Marie Therese's achievement is to have reconciled her devotion to God with her worldliness. The concept of God's presence working in human life, an idea absent from *Lord Weary's Castle*, is presented superbly here. The Mother possesses the ability to minimise contradictions which others tend to polarise into irreconcilable opposites. Essentially, her character is that of the survivor, 'an emigrée in this world and the next', living in the belief that there need be no contradiction between devotion to God and a love of worldly things.

In *Lord Weary's Castle* Lowell was driven by oppositions which he appeared to consider irreconcilable; crucial, large oppositions such as time and eternity, the world and God's kingdom. But in this poem he can come to share the narrator's reverence for the dead nun:

> O mother, here our snuffling crones
> And cretins feared you, but I owe you flowers:
> The dead, the sea's dead, has her sorrows, hours
> On end to lie tossing to the east, cold,
> Without bed-fellows, washed and bored and old,
> Bilged by her thoughts, and worked on by the worms,
> Until her fossil convent come to terms
> With the Atlantic . . . .

The ocean in which the Mother drowned is here God's preserver, not the means of destruction as in 'The Quaker Graveyard in Nantucket'. Comparison with that poem indicates how far Lowell has moved away from the apocalyptic of *Lord Weary's Castle*. The sea here is a kind of purgatory, representing the first step towards full union with God.

The narrator's recognition that the Mother Superior could accept both this world and the spiritual world, rather than seeing them as opposed, leads to a reflection on her own position: 'This sixtieth Christmas, I'm content to pray / For what life's shrinkage leaves from day to day.' Since this poem prefigures Lowell's own acceptance of a limited world in 'Skunk Hour', it is in many respects a crucial turning point. It represents Lowell beginning to consider how contradiction in life is part of the flux of experience: the Mother

Superior can live fully only by living out her apparent contradictions. Randall Jarrell's great admiration of this poem is founded on his recognition of how Lowell has escaped from the limitations imposed by his established voice. Jarrell called 'Mother Marie Therese':

> The most human and tender, the least specialized, of all Mr Lowell's poems; it is warped neither by Doctrine nor by that doctrine which each of us becomes for himself; in it, for once, Mr Lowell really gets out of himself.[9]

The poem is also comparable to Jarrell's own poetry, particularly to the group of poems collected under the title 'The Wide Prospect' (1945). Here, for example, is part of Jarrell's 'An English Garden in Austria':

> By graver stages, up a sterner way,
> You won to those fields the candelabra lit,
> Paused there; sang, as no man since has sung –
> A present and apparent deity – the pure
> Impossible airs of Arcady: and the calm
> Horsehair-wigged shepherds, Gods of that Arcadian
> Academy, wept inextinguishable tears.

The qualities that such a poem shares with 'Mother Marie Therese' are very particular. Jarrell and Lowell both use colloquial rhythmic patterning, and are careful to maintain an apparent conversational flow – a highly skilful use of punctuation is evident to suggest that flow. The tone is kept light enough to prevent the allusions from clogging up the poem, but these help stop the tone from becoming flippant or superficial. Such qualities are characteristic of Jarrell throughout his career: so far they are exceptional to Lowell, but achieved most strikingly in 'Mother Marie Therese'.

I do not wish to imply an influence on Lowell directly from Jarrell. The case is really that Lowell chose Jarrell as an example, since the poetry of both Jarrell and Elizabeth Bishop represented serious and powerful alternatives to his own well-established style. Because Jarrell and Bishop had been uncommitted to the kind of poetry encouraged in the 1940s – the kind created by Schwartz, Roethke, Berryman and Lowell – they became increasingly important to Lowell when that style no longer sufficed for him. Both helped make

available to Lowell the kind of poetry he turned to in *Life Studies.*
However, *The Mills of the Kavanaughs* remains a transitional work.
Generally, in this book, Lowell's themes and attitudes are changing
while his forms and techniques have remained unaltered. The use of
symbol, irony and ambiguity which was so exactly appropriate to
his earlier poetry now hampers his attempt to bring his poetry closer
to human events and experiences. *The Mills of the Kavanaughs* is an
interesting book because of the very reasons why it fails. It is an
important transitional work, and a notable feature is that most of its
characters are themselves considering the problems of timelessness
and time, unity and multiplicity, permanence and flux:

> "Things held together once," she thinks, "But where?
> Not for the life of me! How can I see
> Things as they are, my Love, while April steals
> Through bog and chalk-pit, till these boulders bear
> Persephone – illusory, perhaps,
> Yet her renewal, no illusion . . ."

('The Mills of the Kavanaughs', stanza 6)

Both *The Mills of the Kavanaughs* and *The Dispossessed* were
published during a period when many New Critical ideas
concerning poetry were being reconsidered. Several reviewers
criticised both books on account of their dense, clotted styles.
Randall Jarrell reviewed both books. He looked back at Berryman's
earlier poems – suggesting that they resembled 'statues talking like a
book' – but identified the Nervous Songs as establishing the
elements of an individual style.[10] Berryman's faults were the faults
of influence, but his own voice was beginning gradually to be heard.
Jarrell sensed a similar conflict between voice and inherited style in
The Mills of the Kavanaughs; except that it was the earlier Robert
Lowell who was hampering the emergence and development of the
new. He complained of the 'mannered violence' in the poems, and
suggested that the title poem was like 'an anthology of favourite
Lowell effects'.[11] However, his admiration of 'Mother Marie
Therese' and 'Falling Asleep Over the Aeneid' redeemed the book
for him. So, Berryman is praised since he seems to be finding his
own style; Lowell since he 'gets out' of the established style. Taken
together, the comments provide a fair view of how comfortable
Lowell had been in a New Critical atmosphere, but how this had

tended to oppress Berryman. *The Dispossessed* and *The Mills of the Kavanaughs* were crucial books for Berryman and Lowell. To consider them transitional is to indicate a significant difference between Berryman, Lowell and other middle generation poets. These other poets did not produce any single book that we could consider transitional in the same way. That is, their work does not show the radical stylistic shifts that became a feature of the work of Berryman and Lowell. On the whole, Schwartz, Roethke, Bishop and Jarrell maintain the styles evident in their first books. There is development, of course, but no extreme change. Roethke's later poetry does show a move away from the rigidity of the earlier work, towards the use of a more flexible line length and stanza pattern, but there is no extreme innovation. However, *The Dispossessed* and *The Mills of the Kavanaughs* prepare the way for Berryman and Lowell to make radical reappraisal of their poetry. Perhaps both realised that they could no longer write satisfactorily in those styles. A poetics which had originated as a poetics of recovery could not readily be adapted to deal specifically with loss: it could not suddenly become a 'rhetoric of destitution'.

3

Excellence and Loss

*Does then our lovely rivalry extend beyond
your death? our lovely friendly rivalry
over a quarter-century?
One of my students gives me, late, a long paper
on one of your poems, which I barely can stand
for excellence & loss?*

(Dream Song no. 259)

*They hovered for a moment near discovery,
Figurative enough to see the symbol,
But lacking faith in anything to mean
The same at different times to different people.*

(Robert Frost, 'Maple'.)

The experiences of Berryman and Lowell during the 1950s proved
crucial to the redefinition of their poetics. Such a statement is rather
broad, with a general rather than a specific application. But in
Homage to Mistress Bradstreet (1953) Berryman turned sharply away
from the epistemological basis of his earlier poetics, and began to
explore themes in a different style. It appears probable that personal
traumata underlie the making of *Homage*; as is undoubtedly the case
with *Berryman's Sonnets*, written in 1947 and not published until
1967. In 1955 Berryman wrote his first Dream Song. *Homage* and the
Dream Songs will be examined in the next chapter; here the focus is
on *Life Studies*, though the similarities between Berryman's work
and Lowell's should become apparent. Both the Dream Songs and
Life Studies seek and explore the possibilities of a context in which
personal survival may be achieved amid apparent cultural decline;
and the personal experiences of Berryman and Lowell contribute
greatly to the need for such an exploration. In both works a fresh
poetic emerges. In this chapter I shall examine the individual nature
of Lowell's poetics and the implications this has for an
understanding of his work.

Lowell's divorce from Jean Stafford in 1948 and his marriage to
Elizabeth Hardwick in 1949 signalled and apparently confirmed his
break with the Roman Catholic church. It seemed certain that his
loss of faith precipitated doubts about his poetic talent and
achievement: these would be extreme in a poet whose current
oeuvre was so strongly and seriously committed to a religious
apprehension of experience. The failure of *The Mills of the
Kavanaughs* and the unsympathetic critical reception given to it
seemed to demand of Lowell a change of style. In 1964 he
considered his view of the poems he had written before 1950,
calling them 'symbol-ridden' and 'wilfully difficult', offering
an 'impenetrable surface'. They were characterised as 'prehistoric
monsters', moribund on account of their 'ponderous armor'.[1] What
he was seeking in the 1950s, he wrote, was poetry representing 'a
breakthrough back into life'.[2] The problem of how this was to be
achieved was clearly crucial. One of the striking features of *Life
Studies* is that in most of the poems Lowell does not select and
organise details according to the rigorous principles he had earlier
employed. Many of the poems in *Life Studies* are made up of
associations and details which, although sharply observed, are not
made to correspond with each other according to any consistent
overall pattern or discourse. They are not superbly crafted,
engineered, finished transformations of experience in the style of
Lord Weary's Castle. In many of the poems, metaphors are mixed and
jumbled, ideas and associations are left undeveloped. To recognise
the significance of these features is to begin to realise some of the
methods by which Lowell achieves the 'breakthrough back into life'.
He is less concerned than before to seek or impose patterns of
meanings in experience; the style arises from a more flexible,
inclusive approach. The very title suggests the unfinished quality of
the poems. 'Studies' indicates their particular characteristics – notes
or studies towards a more formal poetry rather than perfected
transformations of experience.

Life Studies has sometimes been considered an isolated
phenomenon, a highly individual book. Its freer rhythms and less
formal style, and Lowell's use of personal, private experience, have
often been seen as part of a radically fresh approach to poetry.
Certainly, the book's tremendous influence needs to be accounted
for. But it is not an isolated book. Other poets of the middle
generation freely used their own lives and childhood experiences as

subjects: Schwartz did so continually, and Roethke did so in *The Lost Son*. Jarrell and Bishop did the same; Jarrell most notably in *The Lost World*, Bishop particularly in her prose. It is true that *Life Studies* goes further in minimising the conventional distance between author and persona, and that the poems of the final section have effects which are largely different from those sought by the other middle generation poets. But similarities are present, and they should alert us to the antecedents that *Life Studies* has.

Some more local influences are also documented. Lowell has made acknowledgement to William Snodgrass, whom he taught in 1953. Snodgrass was then writing the poems that would be collected in *Heart's Needle* (1959), in which he explores the experience of his own divorce. Lowell has similarly acknowledged the importance of the 'Beat' poets in establishing the climate that helped make *Life Studies* possible. The Beats may be considered significant to Lowell because they explicitly rejected the formal academic style of the 1940s. They seemed to restore a distinct energy to poetry, and Lowell was able to use that energy himself. Of course, compared with his own established style, *Life Studies* was revolutionary, almost a fresh start. But in larger terms it succeeded by being part of the movements in poetry during the late 1950s.

The theme of disintegration is the matrix of the book's themes, and is closely associated with the move Lowell makes from his earlier poetics. The book's four parts correspond, though loosely and with some considerable overlap, to four different levels or areas of disintegration. (Steven Yenser's book *Circle to Circle* [Berkeley and Los Angeles: University of California Press, 1975] here needs to be both acknowledged and recommended, since his careful study shows Lowell's great concern for sequence in individual books, and his chapter on *Life Studies* is exceptionally fine.) In the first part of *Life Studies* Lowell is concerned with the break up of cultural order, particularly in religion and politics, and with the positions available to the individual in such break up. In the book's second part, '91 Revere Street', several themes emerge, the most significant being the breakdown of the family and of love. But the sense of cultural paralysis or decline is also present. The focus on the individual's response to larger breakdown continues, but a different possibility is presented. Marie de Medici and the mad negro soldier have already offered individual solutions to breakdown. Lowell's father faces failure in his own way:

He survived to drift from job to job,
to be displaced, to be grimly and
literally that old cliché, a fish out
of water. He gasped and wheezed with
impotent optimism, took on new ideals
with each new job, never ingeniously
enjoyed his leisure, never even hid his
head in the sand.[3]

Part three of *Life Studies* comprises four poems on twentieth-century writers: Lowell examines artistic isolation and alienation within a culture that is itself disintegrating. However, a major concern here is also the survival of the artist, how in these cases isolation can provide the poet with the means of enduring. The fifteen poems which make up the final part of the book, the section actually entitled 'Life Studies', contributed most to the book's impact and influence. As Lowell focuses finally on himself and on his immediate family, the theme of disintegration is fully concentrated upon the individual.

In spite of this four-part division, it is vital to see *Life Studies* as a sequence with particular thematic development. The theme of disintegration does not divide so easily into parts, and the sense of sequence is strong. Charles Altieri believes that the book 'explores the tragedy of decaying fictions', and that it focuses first on shared fictions and finally on the decay of the fiction of self.[4] As a sequence, the book's main movement is towards 'Skunk Hour'. Here the individual finally faces the disintegration of the self with the possibility of suicide, and the consideration of suicide brings together fully the themes of disintegration and survival. While the book is concerned, as are the Dream Songs, with fragmentation on different levels, it is also – again, like the Dream Songs – deeply committed to the individual's ability to survive, to absorb cultural change and to endure.

Since the book is a sequence, 'Beyond the Alps' and 'Skunk Hour' both occupy special places within it. While 'Skunk Hour' focuses finally on how disintegration comes to be concentrated within the individual, 'Beyond the Alps' introduces the theme of cultural break-up. This first poem in the book offers an apology for it, and also begins the close association between cultural disintegration and individual vitality. It is a dense and complex poem, with a wide range of allusions. A strong element in it is concerned with Lowell's turning away from Roman Catholicism, from a world view attempting to achieve or to perceive wholeness, universality and permanence. With the same movement Lowell also turns away from the themes and attitudes of his earlier poetry.

For Lowell, loss of faith involves a loss of the ability to write with confidence in his established style. 'Much against my will, / I left the city of God where it belongs.' Lowell's use of 'will' is important here. One of the poem's central oppositions is between 'will' and the capacity to have an open and flexible attitude towards experience. 'Will' also suggests the style and world view of Lowell's own poetry, the poetry of *Lord Weary's Castle* and *The Mills of the Kavanaughs*. Considering Lowell's first book, Allen Tate once wrote that the 'symbolic language often has the effect of being *willed*'.[5] Jarrell was later to complain of the predominance of will over imagination in *The Mills of the Kavanaughs*.[6] Lowell's relinquishing of such 'willed' poetry, which could be characterised by the desire to unify, select and order objects and details according to a well schematised pattern, begins in *Life Studies*. The jumbles of details and memories comprising many of the poems after 'Beyond the Alps' are very much effects of this relinquishing, and also represent a departure from his religious view, the will to seek permanent and universal unities. 'Beyond the Alps' marks Lowell's acceptance of the inconsistencies of experience. Indeed, the poem represents more than an acceptance of inconsistencies and contradictions: it suggests that these are in some ways essential to modern human experience:

> I envy the conspicuous
> waste of our grandparents on their grand tours –
> long-haired Victorian sages accepted the universe,
> while breezing on their trust funds through the world.

The envy is for a world view that can perceive no contradiction between 'universe' and 'world'. Lowell's envy, though, is ambiguous, for a world view no longer available to him. He implies that the earlier generation could not see the world: the connotations of 'breezing' here suggest a bluff confidence held partly because of material comfort and blinkered vision. The limitations of the grandparents are also indicated by the punning 'trust fund'. Their 'funds' make possible both the grand tour and the comfort of their ideas, their 'trust' in the universal, the absolute. To have that view only, to be unable to see a contradiction or conflict between universe and world is, in spite of Lowell's professed 'envy', ultimately a 'conspicuous waste'.

Generally, 'Beyond the Alps' represents a movement from the limitations of an absolute world view towards the liberation offered by a recognition of the world, of the flux of experience. On the train from God's city – Paris is, by implication, the city of the human – Lowell enacts a kind of rebirth brought about by the very recognition of human limitations, by the realisation that the flux of time liberates humanity even as it condemns everyone to involvement in it.

> Our mountain-climbing train had come to earth.
> Tired of the querulous hush-hush of the wheels,
> the blear-eyed ego kicking in my berth
> lay still, and saw Apollo plant his heels
> On terra firma through the morning's thigh . . .

It is an important poem for Lowell because in the same movement as it comes from the spiritual to the material it clears a space for his new poetics. Because his faith and his poetics had been so involved, Lowell's explicit turning away from Roman Catholicism indicates the need for new poetic strategy. It is not made clear what kind of strategy this will be, and indeed it should be stressed that an alternative poetics is only implied in the poem. 'Beyond the Alps' makes a space in which the rest of *Life Studies* may operate. It suggests the need for a style appropriate to dealing with 'terra firma', with the world's objects, rather than a style appropriate to apprehension of the symbolic qualities of the world's objects.

Although implying Lowell's need for a new poetics, 'Beyond the Alps' fails fully to enact the stylistic breakthrough made by the other poems in *Life Studies*. The train journey is made strongly symbolic – despite Lowell's statement that this is a book without symbols. Lowell also uses puns, a characteristically New Critical technique which had been so effectively part of his earlier style. The cluttered texture and allusions of the second and third stanzas – the third restored to the poem after Berryman's urging – are more typical of the poems preceding 'Beyond the Alps' than of those which follow it. While it prepares the way for *Life Studies*, 'Beyond the Alps' also looks back to the earlier style. Like Lowell between Rome and Paris, the poem is caught at a moment of significant transition.

The final sense that an absolute view of the world is lost is balanced, then, by a sense of gain, a sort of liberation making possible or demanding a different kind of poetry, that would be able thematically and stylistically to accept the flux of experience. In the other poems of this section of *Life Studies*, the individual's capacity to persevere and be stimulated by cultural break up is a significant theme. The other two characters in this part adopt alternative survival strategies when they are divorced from their culture: Marie de Medici by her ability to accept change, the mad negro soldier by utter alienation from his surroundings.

Marie de Medici is, in 'The Banker's Daughter', characterised, like the persona of 'Beyond the Alps', at a time of crucial change. Between the death of her husband Henri IV and the growth of her infant son she is placed outside of society; a condition reinforced, as Lowell notes, by the fact that she is later to be exiled by her son. Yet, like Lowell in 'Beyond the Alps', her capacity for survival is increased by the loss of a fixed position: Lowell emphasises her ability to endure through changing, rather than her failure to resolve or transcend contradictions:

> I rock my nightmare son, and hear him cry
> for ball and sceptre: he asks the queen to die . . .
> And so I press my lover's palm to mine;
> I am his vintage, and his living vine
> entangles me, and oozes mortal wine
> moment to moment. By repeated crime,
> even a queen survives her little time.

Marie de Medici's separation from her culture is echoed by the monologue of the imprisoned mad negro soldier. Though his insanity can be considered a defeat, since it indicates after all his extreme powerlessness in accepting reality, he succeeds too: his success being that of simply enduring on his own terms. The contradictions of his culture and position are for him resolvable only through the total escape that madness represents. Jonathan Raban pointed out how the poem's syntax, with its 'egotistical dislocation', reflects the soldier's success in 'dissolving the outside world altogether'.[7] The nature of the negro's survival shows Lowell examining the various ways that an individual may respond to cultural fragmentation. If the very vitality of the negro is questionable there is however little doubt over Lowell's attitude towards what lies opposite that vitality. Throughout *Life Studies*

Lowell examines the opposition between what is vital and what is static, between what is living and what is paralysed. He comes to celebrate the ability to change, linking it to the capacity to survive. In '91 Revere Street' Lowell writes of how as a child he would try 'to make life stop',[8] and in an important book on Lowell, Vereen Bell has analysed the polarisation of paralysis and flux in this section.[9] Lowell comes, though, to condemn the attempt to 'make life stop', rejecting too the permanence and inflexibility to which it also aspires. In 'Inauguration Day: January 1953', Lowell conveys his mistrust of Eisenhower's administration through images of barrenness and stasis:

> Horseman, your sword is in the groove!
> Ice, ice. Our wheels no longer move;
> Look, the fixed stars, all just alike
> as lack-land atoms, split apart,
> and the Republic summons Ike,
> the mausoleum in her heart.

This polarisation is fairly well defined in *Life Studies*. On one side permanence, the attempt to escape from time, and on the other side a vital acceptance of the passing of time and experience. A search for permanence, for a unified vision, had up to this time been very much present in the work of Lowell, as in Berryman's, as an attempt to escape from time. Berryman used the statute of Humboldt as a reproach to and condemnation of temporality, and used the painting to suggest how the unfortunate human commitment to time might be evaded or transcended. Lowell's use of a religious perespective on experience is part of a comparable attempt to transcend temporal limitation. But the thematic and stylistic thrust of *Life Studies* and the Dream Songs is towards a position in which flux and vitality can be accepted, in which escape from time means only death and paralysis.

At several points in *Life Studies* Lowell introduces ideas which can be read as explorations of the book's poetics. 'Inauguration Day' can be considered such a point, since the implied condemnation of the static and permanent also challenges Lowell's earlier poetic style, and tends to justify the freer, more open poetry of *Life Studies*. Certain parts of '91 Revere Street' may be read in a similar way. This long prose section develops further the theme of the individual's attitude to familial and cultural disintegration. In certain parts Lowell raises the idea of conflict between permanence and change, and these points or moments may be seen as offering a rationale for the poetics of *Life Studies.*

Early in '91 Revere Street' Lowell has been recalling a portrait of his great-great grandfather Mordecai Myers, and this leads him to consider other things which have been 'mislaid past finding':

> There, the vast number of remembered
> *things* remains rocklike. Each is in
> its place, each has its function, its
> history, its drama. There, all is
> preserved by that motherly care one
> either ignored or resented in his
> youth. The things and their owners
> come back urgent with life and
> with meaning – because finished, they
> are endurable and perfect.[10]

In *Nausea* Sartre writes that 'you have to choose: to live or to recount':

> When you are living, nothing happens. The settings change, the people come in and go out, that's all. There are never any beginnings. Days are tacked onto days without rhyme or reason, it is an endless, monotonous addition. . . . That's living. But when you write about life, everything changes; only it's a change nobody notices: the proof of that is that people talk about true stories. As if there could possibly be such things as true stories; events take place one way and we recount them the opposite way. You appear to begin at the beginning . . . in fact you have begun at the end.[11]

The paradigms of literature contradict our sense of how events and experiences occur. Stories, as Sartre indicates, must be shaped to beginnings and ends; and the details of the story are chosen to create a sense of progression from beginning to end. But of course the story's beginning can only be identified when the end is known, the starting point being defined by the nature of the end. However, life is clearly not so shaped to ends and beginnings. One can, for example, only talk of the shape of a life when that life is over. As Coleridge put it in *Table Talk*, when a man is dead, 'his whole life is a matter of history'.

Recognition of this point, here simply made, goes some way towards recognising one of the important challenges of *Life Studies*. In the final section Lowell presents his own life in incidental details and memories. His realisation, implied here as he considers what is 'mislaid past finding', is that the wholeness of an event or life exists only when it is over. He has already sought such endurable perfection but comes in *Life Studies* to refuse it in order to affirm the disordered temporal flux. 'Because they are finished', the things and their owners are indeed 'endurable and perfect'. This perfection is related to the New Critical sense of wholeness of knowledge, of the distanced organised resolution of complexities. It is a perfection and wholeness refuted in *Life Studies*, so the poems themselves are imperfect – and difficult for a reader trained in New Critical idiom. The refusal to order and symbolise experience is strongly linked to refusal of the absolute, the refusal apparent in 'Beyond the Alps'. Lowell comes here to favour a sort of poetry that is not enclosed, that corresponds with and is open to the casual and heuristic associations provided by the interaction of mind and experience. *Life Studies* challenges the idea of poetry as a permanent unified transformation of experience, and enacts deliberate imperfection and incompleteness.

Both *Lord Weary's Castle* and *Life Studies* present views of experience. In the former book Lowell sought a shared and universal view, but in *Life Studies* he presents a self-consciously personal perspective. This perspective is evident at all points, beginning of course in 'Beyond the Alps', where Lowell's personal doubts are placed against the crowd's shared belief in dogma. *Life Studies* is committed to recognising the value of an individual perspective on experience, where *Lord Weary's Castle* sought to define the universal. Earlier, Lowell's Catholicism, or, rather, his religious view of experience generally, meant that he tried to look through experience towards some permanent and universal higher order. In this respect, as has been argued above, the symbol was of central importance, representing an attempt to discover or uncover the spiritual significance of reality, to interpret the world's objects spiritually. Containing contradiction and suggesting the timeless moment, the symbol represented the natural expression of Lowell's desire to seek the numinous in the material.

In Chapter 1 of this study I suggested that for Ransom and Tate the symbol was the essential element of poetic discourse. It transfixed ambiguities and combined knowledge and beauty. It also overcame time. In the poem as act of recovery, the symbol was most important. Comparison of two poems should be instructive, making this idea clear. Roethke's poem 'My Papa's Waltz' is from *The Lost Son*:

> The whiskey on your breath
> Could make a small boy dizzy;
> But I hung on like death:
> Such dancing was not easy.
>
> We romped until the pans
> Slid from the kitchen shelf;
> My mother's countenance
> Could not unfrown itself.
>
> The hand that held my wrist
> Was battered on one knuckle;
> At every step you missed
> My right ear scraped a buckle.
>
> You beat time on my head
> With a palm caked hard by dirt,
> Then waltzed me off to bed
> Still clinging to your shirt.

The poem seems fully to endorse the views Ransom and Tate expressed on symbolism. The dance is the central symbol. It suggests human continuity, and the poem recalls the son's 'dizzy' and rough initiation into the idea that the dance is part of a basic life force. The poem is important in *The Lost Son* because the dance links human energies to the energies evident in the life processes of plants. As continuity, the symbol of the dance results in a kind of recovery of the father. He is found in the memory of the waltz, is recalled and characterised by it. Since the son has been initiated into the dance, he may consider himself as part of its continuity: when the son dances he affirms the presence of the father.

In such ways the symbol in 'My Papa's Waltz' makes the poem's concern the recovery of the father. In *Life Studies*, though, Lowell has denied the power of the symbol to work in this way. 'Father's Bedroom' represents a negation of that supposed power. It is about absence, not presence; about loss, not recovery:

> In my father's bedroom:
> blue threads as thin
> as pen writing on the bedspread,
> blue dots on the curtains,
> a blue kimono,
> Chinese sandals with blue plush straps.
> The broad-planked floor
> had a sandpapered neatness.
> The clear glass bed-lamp
> with a white doily shade
> was still raised a few
> inches by resting on volume two
> of Lafcadio Hearn's
> *Glimpses of unfamiliar Japan.*
> Its warped olive cover
> was punished like a rhinoceros hide.
> In the flyleaf:
> 'Robbie from Mother.'
> Years later in the same hand:
> 'This book has had hard usage
> On the Yangtze River, China.
> It was left under an open
> porthole in a storm.'

Because the father owned these objects he connected them in spite of their being disparate. But at his death the connection they had is lost. With his absence they are in the poem as mere unrelated objects. Roethke restored and affirmed the connection the waltz made between son and father. Lowell's poem has no such centre, no symbolic meaning or presence that can unite the things in the bedroom. It has no symbol which unifies, which restores these 'lost connections'. Roethke brings everything together: the whiskey, the pans, the mother's face, the father's 'battered' and dirty hand, his belt and shirt. These have meaning because the central symbol, the waltz, involves them all. They become included in the connection between humans and elemental forces, the link that the waltz symbolises. But 'Father's Bedroom' lacks this link, this connecting symbol. The objects seem futile, meaningless. Lowell has recognised that symbolic discourse relies on presence, on centre: to write of loss and absence the symbolic mode has to be interrupted, negated.

In *Life Studies* Lowell repudiates not only the symbolist technique, but also the religious apprehension of experience that was for him closely involved with the symbol. The ideas of Hopkins regarding instress and inscape are by now remote: Lowell no longer seeks a higher, spiritual order through examination of the apparent material order. He now recognises the intransigence of the material, that it neither reveals or conceals symbolic or spiritual order. In 'Father's Bedroom' the list of objects does not amount to a symbolic discourse representative of the dead father; the things merely exist on a material level. It is the very intransigence of these things as things that is emphasised, the poem's pathos in a large measure deriving from the endurance of things (in spite of their 'hard usage') while their owner is dead. But the poem's powerful sadness comes also from another source, that is, from the very technique Lowell uses. For, sadly and terribly, the things just remain things, stubbornly and grimly resisting the poetic impulse that would give them meaning by turning them into metonyms or metaphors or symbols. The tremendously influential Coleridgian idea of the transformative and esemplastic power of the imagination seems here to be denied utterly. Perhaps this is why these poems are so sad and comfortless and painful. The imagination seeks to order experience and give it meaning. Order, meaning: these are so humanly comforting, but things as merely things are so devoid of comfort. In 'Father's Bedroom', as in 'Water' from *For the Union Dead*, Lowell's imagination cannot act on memory or on things to give them a comforting meaning. The poem exists as it does because of Lowell's inability to discover or create meaning in objects – he is forced to accept the materiality of the world rather than condemn it as a 'land of unlikeness'. He finds here an involvement with the incidental objects of experience.

The freer rhythms and more open poems of *Life Studies* reflect Lowell's more flexible attitude to experience. Events are not considered from a rigid perspective but from a fairly fluid, shifting one. In 'My Last Afternoon With Uncle Devereux Winslow', for example, the drifting sensibility and large variety of objects mentioned are results of Lowell's refusal to control or order experience from a single fixed perspective. It is as though he is prepared to allow objects some movement, some freedom to act upon him. He does not simply force them into his preconceived pattern.

In *Life Studies* the attitude to art which Lowell begins to form involves certain contradictions. There is an apparent mistrust of the distance which his earlier poetry had created between itself and experience, of poetic paradigms that are ontologically distinct from the other available forms of discourse and knowledge. One impulse of *Life Studies* is towards an openness of form. Lowell implies that the formalist poetry of his earlier style threatens the very openness, the flux, of experience. If the sort of poetry encouraged by the New Criticism was, as Paul Bové has put it, a 'defensive troping against time',[12] then Lowell is moving away from that and towards an acceptance of time and disorder. The idea of art actually threatening life becomes strongest in Lowell's last books. Yet his trust in art as a means of momentarily defining and ordering experience is also powerfully present there. In *History*, as in the Dream Songs, writing is a means of creating and sustaining life: the threat then is that if one stops writing, one also stops living. Writing becomes a way of temporarily creating order from the chaos of experience, and Lowell recognises the ambivalence of this temporary ordering. While the capacity to order is essential to the human spirit, the orderer or artist is no longer being true to experience. In *Life Studies* Lowell suggests the possibilities of order while making the reader experience the ambivalences of such order. His texts give order yet displace themselves as they at once explore and resist their own capabilities.

The implications of these ideas can be seen quite fully in 'Skunk Hour'. However, such dualist attitudes to art's relationship with experience begin to be apparent in the third part of *Life Studies*. The ambivalence is linked to the theme of survival, as the four writers in this section are each considered to be enduring through art. Ford Madox Ford, Santayana, Delmore Schwartz and Hart Crane are each outside of society, lonely, seemingly helpless, alienated figures. But in each case a kind of survival is achieved through their ability to internalise problems and contradictions and order them in the creation of their art. In the case of Crane and Schwartz the achieved survival is tenuous and ambiguous.

'Ford Madox Ford' provides a view of Ford's position in society. He is alienated from the ministers, from the soldiers alongside whom he fights, and from post-war London, by the fact that he is an artist. As an exile, his final alienation is from his dwindling audience. In spite of the emphasis on this alienation, this divorce, the poem ends with a quite straightforward recognition of Ford's qualities, as though it is left to another artist, Lowell, to reunite Ford with those things from which he has been gradually separated. Lowell praises Ford because he possessed charity, a simple human virtue. He does not praise Ford's art but his human quality, as though it is this which can effect his return to the society from which his art has alienated him.

At the end of the poem there is an achieved transparency of language, a straightforwardness that highlights the loose casual nature of the preceding poetry. Closing with a simple declarative sentence, there is a sudden recognition which breaks through the wandering allusive poem and transforms it:

> Fiction! I'm selling short
> your lies that made the great your equals.
> Ford,
> you were a kind man and you died in want.

The fictionality of anecdote is introduced partly because of Ford's renown for telling far-fetched tales, a reputation already acknowledged by Lowell in recounting the poem's first anecdote. Lowell recognises that even the supposed truth which anecdotes and personal references supply is fictive; as Sartre pointed out, there is no such thing as a true story. But that recognition here moves the poem to its close, as though one can actually trust art at the moment when its fictionality is recognised; as though an actual wary transparency is available with the recognition that in spite of its distancing paradigms art is also open to honesty and integrity.

The divorce of the writer from culture is even more extreme in the case of Santayana. He has outlived his achievements to the extent that people are surprised to find him alive. His utter separation from his surroundings is highlighted by his being an atheist dying in a convent where the nuns pray daily for his soul. The specific problem that Santayana must face, the contradiction with which he must somehow come to terms, is how he can accept the necessary physical care provided by the nuns (care which for them is inseparable from spiritual care) yet maintain his atheism. He can only satisfy the uneasiness caused by this contradiction through his ability to transform and contain it by a literary device. He thus expresses his religious position in terms that can be seen as ambiguous and paradoxical: 'There is no God and Mary is His Mother.' The absurdity satisfies, since through it he can balance, without the need for resolution, the contradictions of his old age.

Hart Crane too survives through his art, and through his ability to create a role for himself. This role, like his art, both alienates him from society and helps him to maintain his identity and existence: Lowell chooses to present Crane some time before his suicide, presumably before bravado had turned into despair. In this dramatic monologue Crane can maintain a fierce pride in the role he has assumed, and in doing so challenges the reader into a deeper emotional involvement with his poetry: 'Who asks for me, the Shelley of my age, / must lay his heart out for my bed and board.' The couplet is important in the sequence, directly preceding the strongly personal poems of 'Life Studies'. However, this third section has a much more general significance for the sequence, establishing as it does the idea that art is a means of continuing existence, of affirming the self.

Since Lowell's view of art as a means of ordering chaotic experience might here seem to be somewhat consistent with the ideas of Ransom and Tate, several important differences need to be identified. For Ransom and Tate art existed as a systematic organisation of values and experience, and its aim was recovery and preservation. But for Lowell art's organisation is personal and momentary, rather than shared, systematic and permanent. This view of art emerges more fully in *History*, as it does for Berryman in the Dream Songs, but it is also here in *Life Studies*. The poems of the final section are discomforting for several reasons, but a large amount of the discomfort results from Lowell's technique, rather than from the subject-matter. In poems such as 'My Last Afternoon With Uncle Devereux Winslow' and 'Sailing Home From Rapallo' (these strike me as the strongest examples of a technique employed generally in the 'Life Studies' section), Lowell disrupts the authorial capacity to order from a fixed and settled perspective on experience. He cannot come to terms with the death in 'Sailing Home From

Rapallo' and so there is a failure to resolve the issue for the reader. The poem itself is in flux, and disallows any easy or comforting resolution of its discordant elements. The misspelling with which the poem ends, '*Lowell* had been misspelled *LOVEL*', indicates a variety of ideas. It sharply defines the mother's loneliness and isolation in Italy; the poem had begun with a similar emphasis. But, like the objects in the father's bedroom, the misspelling also indicates absence. The mother is no longer present to control or correct the spelling of her name: her necessary absence from the poem makes the misspelling appropriate. The poems of *Life Studies* are disturbing because their ontology points very specifically to human inability to control time, the flux of experience, death. Lowell relinquishes the attempt to escape, transcend or dominate these things, and through necessity attempts to accept flux and imperfection.

In a great deal of Lowell's poetry there is a fascination with art's temporary orderings, with the aesthetic impulse. There is an emphasis on the need for expression, however inadequate, provisional, or even absurd that expression may be. This emphasis lies behind Lowell's use of details from his personal life in this final section. M. L. Rosenthal tended to misdirect profitable debate in this area with his description of these poems as 'confessional'. It is true that the sense of relief caused by self-exposure in this book was important to Lowell. In a letter quoted by Rosenthal, this is made very clear: 'Something not to be said again was said. I feel drained, and know nothing except that the next outpouring will have to be unimaginably different.'[13] However, to suggest that the achievement of such relief was the impulse behind *Life Studies* would be seriously misleading, placing too great an emphasis on what is only one feature of a complex style. Lowell's treatment of his own life in time is deeply involved with his rejection of New Critical views on poetry's epistemological status.

The final section of *Life Studies* moves well away from the idea that art is unchanging, that it offers 'concrete' knowledge, and that it can be situated beyond time. The constant presence of a personal perspective – which itself shifts – never allows the reader to forget the personally relative perspective that governs and underlies knowledge, making it provisional. Lowell and Berryman later strongly emphasised the personal relativity of knowledge in *History*, *Homage to Mistress Bradstreet* and the Dream Songs. History and experience become highly self-conscious personal creations, and almost become personal property. Meaning is personal and relative, events being seen from one point in time. In *Life Studies* Lowell tends to stress the relativity of knowledge. The idea that established fictions can lose their validity and may need to be replaced or redefined has been raised in the book's very first poem. Since *Life Studies* is a sequence, it is important to consider the differences between 'Beyond the Alps' and 'Skunk Hour'. In the first poem Lowell appears reluctant to accept temporal change, but in the last poem he has come to affirm that very dynamism.

In '91 Revere Street' the lost things came back because they were finished: perfectly stored in memory, they were closed to change. But as they endured because they were no longer alive, Lowell, on the other hand, can endure in 'Skunk Hour' because of his acceptance of change. He can accept a time-bound existence; also, most importantly, he can articulate. In this poem the ability to describe and give temporary meaning to experience is the source of Lowell's capacity to persevere against the destruction of the self. Generally, critics and readers of the poem have agreed that what Lowell called the poem's 'ambiguous' affirmation derives from the skunks. However, this is not strictly the case, since the ambiguous affirmation must exist at a more fundamental level. It is achieved at the moment when Lowell can in this poem provide the skunks with a meaning which in reality they do not possess. His survival, his resistance of the self-destructive impulse, is achieved because of his restored capacity to give meaning to the world's objects and to derive comfort from that capacity. The affirmation is ambiguous because on the very terms on which it exists it must be ambiguous: the transformation of the skunks being self-consciously temporary and personal.

Life Studies has explored the failure of the imagination to give order and meaning to objects and experiences, the failure to transform reality. Yet in the end Lowell's survival is engineered by a fiction, by the temporary restoration of his lost esemplastic power. The line 'my mind's not right' and the following stanza represent a nadir. But then Lowell introduces the skunks, suggesting the presence of disinterested care in the world, and providing a kind of reproach to the introverted narrator. Thus Lowell interprets the skunks' actions in a self-conscious way, giving meaning to them. This ability of momentarily transforming reality through language and imagination becomes fused with the ability to endure. The skunks are fictions.

However, it is not true that *Life Studies* just enacts or rehearses the trading of one myth or fiction for another: Lowell turning from Roman Catholicism to faith in the imagination. Lowell is conscious of the fictionality of his skunks, and makes this evident by foregrounding them with lines such as 'my mind's not right' and 'I myself am hell'. These self-reflective, self-absorbed lines – in which Lowell identified the 'rhetoric of destitution' – serve to emphasise how far his skunks are fictive, relying for meaning on his personal and temporary perspective. In fact, J. F. Nims went some way towards recognising this when he expressed an alternative imaginative transformation. Lowell's lines read:

> . . . skunks, that search
> in the moonlight for a bite to eat.
> They march on their soles up Main Street:
> white stripes, moonstruck eyes' red fire
> under the chalk-dry and spar spire
> of the Trinitarian Church.

This was how Lowell prepared for the affirmation of the final stanza. Nims proposed an alternative, and his cynical view of the skunks reinforces the idea that it is not the skunks but the power of the imagination that forms the basis for the poem's affirmative qualities:

> Flat-footed skunks that prowl
> In the lewd moon to stuff their gut;
> Up Main Street, stinking-proud they strut.[14]

In fact, a fairly contentious point might be introduced here: that even if 'Skunk Hour' had closed by presenting such a cynical view of the skunks, an affirmation would still be there, since it is the very ability to give meaning to experience that is being affirmed in the poem.

'Skunk Hour' anticipates the attitude to poetry evident in *History* and the Dream Songs. I will examine later how Berryman and Lowell have a fascination with the ordering of poetry, fascination equally balanced but at times cruelly outweighed by their recognition of its inadequacy as a means of dealing with experience. I suggested earlier that one effect of *Life Studies* is to make the reader experience the ambivalence of order, and in the work of Berryman and Lowell this ambivalence is to become increasingly pronounced.

4

History and Seduction

history is inaccessible to us except in textual form

(Jameson, *The Political Unconscious*)

You're gone; I am learning to live in history.
What is history? What you cannot touch.

(Lowell, 'Mexico')

out of the maize and air
your body's made, & moves. I summon, see
from the centuries it.
I think you won't stay.

(Berryman, *Homage to Mistress Bradstreet*)

In reviewing *77 Dream Songs* Lowell looked back over Berryman's career and wrote that *Homage to Mistress Bradstreet* was 'the most resourceful historical poem in our literature'.[1] This claim might appear odd, seeming to reflect Lowell's own preoccupation with history rather than any prominent feature of Berryman's work. But there is a lot of truth in the idea. While *Homage* is original and challenging in many ways, it is most astonishing in the relationship it creates between Berryman and Anne Bradstreet, between the present and the past; or, to put it in Lowell's terms, between historian and resource. It is not just an attitude to history, but an attitude also to time, loss and writing, since historiography involves these. *Homage*, the Dream Songs and *History* are intensely concerned with time, loss and writing, and the ideas and attitudes examined in these works represent the fullest poetic development of Berryman and Lowell.

At a celebrated moment in *Homage* Berryman enters the poem and begins a dialogue with Anne Bradstreet. This dialogue continues for some time, and Berryman and Anne Bradstreet become lovers. Berryman's act of seduction is completed. There are many ideas

70

implied in this section of dialogue and seduction. Clearly, one major result of the action is to place emphasis on the fictionality of history. The act of seduction becomes analogous to the act of creating history, and relates that act also to the act of making poetry. The present seduces the past, and in leading it away brings it to the present. This is precisely what Berryman does in the whole of *Homage*, as this movement of seduction implies. With it he emphasises how our sense of history relies upon the needs or demands of the present, how the creation of history is an analogue of literary creation. The present creates history; the meaning of history does not exist independently of the present. History's meaning is relational.

Two further points need to be made. In an essay Berryman said that he entered the poem in order to give Anne Bradstreet a more intensely physical presence – in effect, to make her real.[2] One of the problems present in the writing of the poem, Berryman points out, was of making the narrator and Anne Bradstreet 'in some measure physically present to each other'. For him the dialogue and seduction provided a solution to this problem. But the poem actually produces the opposite effect. For in entering it Berryman does not make Anne Bradstreet more real – he fictionalises himself. In the poem both Berryman and Bradstreet are very consciously fictionalised. Berryman in the poem has fallen for the product of his own fictional ability. He falls in love with his own creation. Pygmalion's love for the statue made it come to life; but here it is as though Berryman must become fictional in order to love Anne; as though Pygmalion could consummate his love for the statue only through becoming statuesque. It is quite clear in the poem that Berryman creates a fictional Anne Bradstreet, and is rather out of sympathy with the 'historical' Bradstreet. He cannot accept her faith, and even finds her poetry to be of little worth: 'all this bald/abstract didactic rime I read appalled/harrassed for your fame'. But in creating an alternative Bradstreet, a fictive one, he can fall in love with her. In doing so he must also make himself fictive: thus the association of seduction, history and fiction becomes comprehensive.

Homage is a poem in which history-making is considered explicitly as an analogue to literary creation, and both are investigated through the metaphor of seduction. Berryman stresses how history is relative to the present, not absolute in itself. Thus Anne Bradstreet has to be 'summoned' in order to have a relationship to the present, and Berryman must be there as a self-conscious twentieth-century narrator. This is all a long way from the sense of history Berryman had provided in his earlier work. In 'Winter Landscape' art could transcend time and history, but in *Homage* the impulse to make art concurs more completely with the impulse to make history. History is made in the same way that art is made. Opposed to the views put forward in 'Winter Landscape', here time, history and art have each become relative and interrelated for Berryman, rather than absolute and distinct.

Lowell's remark on *Homage* was published in 1964, when he himself was beginning to explore the relation between history and poetry. Lowell had of course long been considered a poet who used history partly to remind the present of the demands and achievements of the past. Jarrell once wrote that Lowell looked on history as Blücher looked on London: as something marvellous to plunder.[3] But Lowell had not presented history self-consciously, and does not appear to have considered it as created by an impulse and process comparable to the aesthetic impulse and process. His historical poems tended to be monologues, or to incorporate historical values in order to produce a contrast with the present. But as Berryman did, Lowell comes more to use the past, to create history in a self-consciously aesthetic way. In *For the Union Dead* (1964) he used historical events and values much more uncertainly than he had in his earlier work. In the much acclaimed title poem, for example, Lowell wavers between being entrapped by history and liberated by it. The past exists as a legacy that the present has failed to deserve, and in losing it has lost a sense of worth. But the past is also there as a legacy which is suspicious or even repugnant; a past that the present has done well to evade. This duality of attitudes never emerges so fully in the poem that it becomes simply ambivalent; and they are in any case made intricate by Lowell's continual dislocation of time perspectives. It is as though Lowell has failed, has at once lost the ability to judge the present, control the past and produce comforting aesthetic form. Of course, 'failure' is a misleadingly pejorative term, since it is precisely this 'failure' that makes the poem successful and gives 'For the Union Dead' its greatness. Lowell has circumvented what Roland Barthes called 'the euphoria of the preterite'. Barthes used this phrase in *Writing Degree Zero* when considering how use of the past tense implies comforting distance from and dominance over the past. A sense of well-being, euphoria, results from the apparent capacity to control time, as signified by the preterite. In 'For the Union Dead' Lowell challenges such euphoria by disrupting tense.

For the Union Dead certainly signalled a change in Lowell's attitude towards history, in that he was beginning to provide a firmer sense of the relationship between history and creativity. Although *Near the Ocean* does not explore this relationship in so direct a way, it is a powerful theme in *History*. This book had a long and almost notorious genesis. In 1969 Lowell published *Notebook 1967–68*. It was a radical departure for him: a series of poems, all of fourteen lines, collectively making a kind of Lowellian diary of events and ideas (both quotidian and apocalyptic) for the years 1967 and 1968. Lowell then revised and expanded this book – according, as he said, to an alternative pattern – and published it in 1970 as *Notebook*. He then went on to revise *Notebook*, once again altering the overall pattern, to the extent of making it into two books published in 1973: *History* and *For Lizzie and Harriet*. These were published simultaneously, along with his new sequence, *The Dolphin*; all using the fourteen-line form throughout.

These goings on irritated reviewers and critics, some of whom argued that the revisions often worsened individual poems. Lowell himself was rather defensive – in *Notebook* he wrote 'I am sorry to ask anyone to buy this book twice,' but then he asked his readers to buy it a third time, as *History* and *For Lizzie and Harriet*. Critics were also rather unimpressed by Lowell's apparent abnegation of his immense technical skill. The fourteen-liners were often scarcely sonnets, and were not disciplined according to any consistent structural principle. The poet renowned for his skill was certainly letting his audience down. Also, very few of the poems stood up very well individually. The book's effect was cumulative, and as a book not as a series of individual poems. I think what Ian Hamilton, among others, suggests, is here perfectly true. Lowell had seen in the Dream Songs a variety of fresh possibilities, and was keen to explore them in his own work: in particular this sense that the cumulative effect could be more important than any individual part of the work.[4] The use of a set form was obviously important too, as it had been for Berryman, enabling him to write without feeling the need to create an individual form for each poem, and to place emphasis upon a larger sense of structure.

The use of the long poem itself distinguishes Berryman and Lowell from other middle generation poets. *History* and the Dream Songs belong to the American long poem tradition that was continued by Pound, Crane, Williams and Olson. The long poem was largely ignored by Schwartz, Roethke, Jarrell and Bishop. True, Schwartz did complete and publish the first book of his planned epic, *Genesis*, in 1943. But he abandoned this project and today remains familiar mainly through his shorter poems. Roethke consistently used sequences of four or more related poems, but these cannot be compared to the ambitious long works of Berryman and Lowell. There is a kind of audacity evident in these long works, considered even as a direct challenge to Eliot and Pound. 'Maybe hostility keeps us going', wrote Berryman when considering *Homage to Mistress Bradstreet* as an attempt to evade the style of *The Waste Land*.[5] This hostility does appear to have been an impulse behind the Dream Songs and *History*. Again, the idea of challenging the modernists, the desire to struggle against influence in this way, is a major difference between Berryman, Lowell and the other middle generation poets.

Broadly speaking, *History*'s major concern is with the self's conscious apprehension of disordered experience, and the concomitant attempt to systematise such experience. In the books from which *History* is partly made, Lowell had attempted different arrangements of the material, different sorts of order. In *Notebook 1967–68* he used the framework of a year, and thus had a straightforwardly chronological apprehension of events. In *Notebook*, though, he rejected this and tried to find a more intuitive but aesthetic arrangement: 'my plot rolls with the seasons, but one year is confused with another.' Lowell was also careful to avoid a too highly schematised pattern, warning that the poems do not amount to a 'sequence of related material'.

For *History* Lowell used a more sweeping chronological order than before. However, the formation here is not that of a year in the life of Lowell, as in *Notebook 1967–68*, but of Lowell's conception of his life in history. History finally provides the book's sense of order and progression, but history is considered throughout from a self-consciously twentieth-century perspective. It was precisely this which made many reviewers uneasy: the sheer audacity of creating history from a single consciousness. Clive James pointed out that everything that had taken place 'since the dawn of humanity' tended to appear as something happening to Lowell.[6] In an extremely hostile review (for which he later wrote a verse apology), Peter Dale made a similar point: history for Lowell seems to be an 'inflated and conflated' view of 'Romantic figures', all used as 'vague precursors of Lowellian angst'.[7]

In both of the reviews here quoted there is much that is perfectly valid. In Lowell's arrangement history is a self-conscious creation by and around his own consciousness. What made the reviewers uneasy was the personal assimilation of history. But one of the most challenging and most important features of *History* is precisely this sense that our history is the result of an aesthetic instinct, a desire for order. Lowell demonstrates how this aesthetic need for a sustained and consistent arrangement lies under our making of a historical order, and both are part of our attempt to refute a disordered series of events. In *History*, then, history is formed by Lowell's consciousness, and Lowell himself is very much there, reminding us that this is his formation. But Lowell's selection, and the way that it is a self-consciously Lowellian selection, invites us seriously to examine concepts such as a shared history and the past as legacy.

We are often reminded – for example, by Frank Kermode in *The Genesis of Secrecy* – that there is an ambiguous and sometimes uneasy relationship between the interpretive act and historical situation.[8] The present both makes possible and limits interpretation of the past. The demands of the present invite us to seek analogies or different kinds of order in the past, to select what we need from history. But of course, that selection is both a freedom and a limitation. Our present determines our view of the past, thus making it at once liberated and limited. A similar movement between possibility and restriction is one force behind Lowell's formation of history. For as one accepts its essentially personal nature, one also accepts it as essentially provisional. At the same time, though, one also sees the possibilities of history – it is not only open to change, it must change as the single consciousness must move through time.

The idea that history is being changed as the consciousness changes has important results in *History*. Since these poems are orderings of experience, it follows that these must always be provisional. The consciousness from which they are created is always open to change. On a simple level this comes to mean that no poem is a satisfactory fixed achievement. As the consciousness shifts, through changes, or just through time, the poems, Lowell suggests, must be revised if they are to remain of any value to the consciousness which created them. Such openness to revision is of course prominent in the genesis of *History* and *For Lizzie and Harriet*. In *Notebook* Lowell wrote that he had handled his published book 'as if it were a manuscript'. And *Notebook* itself would become another manuscript. Poems for him have become like drafts or manuscripts; they are not immortal, timeless, complete in themselves. Charles Lamb once expressed his horror at seeing the hand-written drafts of 'Lycidas': they suggested that Milton's words were 'mortal, alterable, displaceable'. He was so horrified that he resolved 'never to go into the workshop of any great artist again', and wrote that he found even handwriting 'repugnant'.[9] But for Lowell words have become precisely 'mortal, alterable, displaceable': he has opened up his drafts and his 'workshop' to the public. In spite of those who, like Lamb, would prefer to consider poetry as immortal and beyond time, Lowell has become dedicated to poems as time-bound, as well as transient and replaceable: as being handwritten rather than published.

There is also in *History* a mistrust of the very value of human knowledge. As we have seen, from the start of their careers, Berryman and Lowell were keen to follow the idea that the poem is a formulation of knowledge which overcomes time. They would certainly have subscribed to Ransom's view that the poet 'perpetuates in his poem an order of existence' which, outside and beyond the poem, is 'constantly crumbling beneath his touch'.[10] But in their later work Berryman and Lowell are asking what can be perpetuated whole when the reader and writer are themselves constantly in flux. Ransom's view is made plausible by his desire for an art which would defeat time. But in *History* and the Dream Songs poems are time-bound, committed to time and change as their authors are. *History* particularly is open to revision as Lowell himself moves through time to the position of a different reader or a different creator. If poetry is still knowledge for Berryman and Lowell then both poetry and knowledge are now relative, not absolutes.

Such concerns are evident in one of *History*'s most celebrated poems, 'The Nihilist as Hero':

> "All our French poets can turn an inspired line;
> who has written six passable in sequence?"
> said Valery. That was a happy day for Satan . . .
> I want words meat-hooked from the living steer,

but a cold flame of tinfoil licks the metal log,
beautiful unchanging fire of childhood
betraying a monotony of vision . . .
Life by definition breeds on change,
each season we scrap new cars and wars and women.
But sometimes when I am ill or delicate,
the pinched flame of my match turns unchanging green,
a cornstalk in green tails and seeded tassel . . .
A nihilist has to live in the world as is,
gazing the impassible summit to rubble.

Like many others in the book, this poem may be considered as an
exploration of – even an apology for – the principles on which
History is based. Lowell begins by implying a rejection of poetry as
inspiration. 'I want words meat-hooked from the living steer':
Lowell's hope is that his words could be mortal living parts of
reality. The very vivid metaphor indicates an act of violent theft, and
emphasises that appropriation. Lowell wants his words to be stolen
from the living; not to be considered the result of happy inspiration.
This desire, though, is then challenged by Lowell's knowledge that
words coldly fix meaning; taken from the living steer, they turn out
to be dead things, cooked, not raw. The words that attempt
somehow to assimilate reality are static and lifeless. The child's
reassuring belief in permanence, though, is another self-deception,
a 'monotony of vision', that attempts to deny the fact of mutability.
A conflict begins to emerge, and it is a crucial conflict in *History*; the
refusal to consider change against the willingness to accept it. Here
Lowell suggests that his words can live only because of a recognition,
on the part of reader and writer, of their provisional status, of their
necessary openness to revision, of their transient condition.

The poem here also raises Lowell's fear that he will be 'fixed'.
When ill he fears that his life and work will be fixed patterns, in the
way that death puts a life into a pattern: when a man is dead, 'his
whole life is a matter of history'. Lowell is afraid of the freezing
effected by such closure. The fear is strongly connected to a fear of
death, but it is also a fear that his words will have lost this openness
to revision. In fact, Elizabeth Bishop's 1978 poem, 'North Haven',
which she wrote in memory of Lowell, concentrates finally on this
point. Lowell's death means the inability to change: both the words
and his life are stilled:

You can't derange, or re-arrange,
Your poems again. (But the Sparrows can their song.)
The words won't change again. Sad friend, you cannot change.

However, the fear of life ending when the capacity to revise ends, is reduced in 'The Nihilist as Hero' as Lowell concludes with the possibilities offered by the nihilist. A nihilist may be characterised by the refusal to accept value, by a refutation of given objective validity. In such ways, Lowell's *History* is nihilistic; he denies the fixing of values and condemns the monotony of vision. With all its creations and re-creations, *History* emphasises the provisionality of words and values. The poem ends with the nihilist as someone who sees rubble not mountains. This seems to offer to Lowell a solution to his fear that his work would be unchanging. To the nihilist his work would not be a mountain, a frozen 'impossible summit', with a fixed meaning. If his readers have understood, they will read nihilistically, recognising that the work is provisional, built from rubble and open always to rearrangement, reinterpretation. It is as though after Lowell's death his poems will live, survive, only if the nihilistic reader can ensure and affirm their capacity for change.

In this study I have already mentioned Eliot's famous complaint about how words are liable to crack and break. Earlier it was relevant because it expressed brilliantly a complaint that Berryman and Lowell echoed. They too wished that words could freeze the living moment, arrest the flux of experience. They both sought themes and expressed attitudes uncommitted to the temporal; Lowell a permanent religious faith, Berryman art that could be symbolised through painting and statue: art forms not dependent on time. But here Lowell has almost reversed the terms of Eliot's lament. 'The Nihilist as Hero', along with other poems in *History*, expresses a kind of delight in the fact that words do decay, do perish, cannot stay still or stay in place: 'imperfection is the language of art'. Imperfection has become a source of celebration, of vitality. It is the dread that words could fix that here horrifies Lowell: thus the nihilist ends up as a hero.

However, more than poetry is represented by the 'impossible summit'. Lowell indicates that humans should be aware of the transience of knowledge; knowledge as a provisional and temporary means of systematising the chaotic. The mountain of knowledge is also rubble. 'Rubble', the poem's last word, is very important. It suggests what is left after destruction, and what is available for rebuilding. Knowledge and values can be seen as relative, as constructs open to rearrangement or destruction, but which can also be created fresh from the same rubble. In just this way Lowell has made rubble out of his own books, out of *Notebook 1967–68* and *Notebook*: here he reminds us that *History* too is rubble.

Lowell's admiration of Wallace Stevens had been long and deeply held. Lowell himself has acknowledged an affinity between Stevens' poetry and *Notebook*.[11] Stevens' major concern is with the human imaginative capacity for structuring reality, a capacity that attains its highest level in art. In his later work Stevens often develops the idea that such organisations need continually to be redefined and restructured. The second part of *Notes Towards A Supreme Fiction*, which is entitled 'It Must Change', is of special relevance to *History*; indeed, either of those titles could be used to reflect some central ideas in *History*.

This part of *Notes* includes a section focused on the statue of 'General Du Puy', and when Lowell reviewed *Transport to Summer* in 1947, he enthusiastically chose this section for scrutiny.[12] For Stevens the absurdity of the statue lies in its immobility, the 'true flesh' on which it was modelled having become 'inhuman bronze':

> a permanence, so rigid,
> That it made the General a bit absurd,
>
> Changed his true flesh to an inhuman bronze.
> There never had been, never could be, such
> A man. The lawyers disbelieved, the doctors
>
> Said that as keen, illustrious ornament,
> As a setting for geraniums, the General,
> The very Place du Puy, in fact, belonged
>
> Among our more vestigial states of mind.
> Nothing had happened because nothing had changed.
> Yet the General was rubbish in the end.

There is a close relationship between Stevens' rubbish and Lowell's rubble. It is worth noting too that Lowell had described the making of *History* as a series of acts 'cutting the waste marble from the figure'.[13] The metaphor at once indicates two important things; that the form of *History* is achieved by an act that combines destruction and creation, and the form is not itself final, since the book may be reshaped through the same activity that led to its present form. The Dream Songs perform a similarly deconstructive act. Berryman is dismantling Humboldt's statue, and making the Dream Songs from the rubble of his earlier work. He undermines the concept of an art beyond time, and from Humboldt's bronze statue attempts the 'true flesh' of Henry.

Such an approach to 'The Nihilist as Hero' may introduce another of *History*'s major concerns; that is, the relationship which Lowell identifies between his life and his art. At certain points in the book there is the belief that the act of writing is the act of making Lowell's life. *History* is Lowell's creation of himself in history – as well as the forming of history through himself. The aesthetic ordering becomes an act of self creation, as it undoubtedly does for Berryman in the Dream Songs. The idea occurs again and again in *History* and the Dream Songs; writing as the means of surviving, and the means of making a life. Elizabeth Bishop also explored this association in 'Crusoe in England', from *Geography III* (1976). Shipwrecked and alone, Crusoe can survive only through making his memory and imagination act upon the materials accidentally provided. Bishop implies a view of the artist similar to that presented by Stevens. The imaginative structuring of reality is essential to Crusoe as it is fundamental to the artist. The orderings of Berryman and Lowell are basic to their continuing survival. '*Question: why do I write? Answer: if I stop, / I might as well stop breathing*' Lowell writes in 'Abstraction'. The idea emerges more fully in 'Reading Myself':

> Like thousands, I took just pride and more than just,
> struck matches that brought my blood to a boil;
> I memorized the tricks to set the river on fire –
> somehow never wrote something to go back to.
> Can I suppose I am finished with wax flowers
> and have earned my grass on the minor slopes of
>   Parnassus . . .
> No honeycomb is built without a bee
> adding circle to circle, cell to cell,
> the wax and honey of a mausoleum –
> this round dome proves its maker is alive;
> the corpse of the insect lives embalmed in honey,
> prays that its perishable work live long
> enough for the sweet-tooth bear to desecrate –
> this open book . . . my open coffin.

Books can only be open when the process of writing is closed or finished. Lowell's fear is that when the pattern is completed, his work finished, then his life too will be over. The life, frozen into the pattern, will now be understandable to the reader, able now to see it as a whole, as an ordered finished arrangement. But since that organisation may only be revealed at death, the open book is also the open coffin. As noted above, in 'North Haven' Elizabeth Bishop located the sadness of Lowell's death precisely here. Her closing words, 'Sad friend, you cannot change', are richly ambiguous. They can suggest at once Lowell's inability to change his words and to change himself. Such inability to change has been the threat faced by Lowell throughout *History*, and one can see how the revisions, the refusals to fix the pattern, became his assurance that he would go on living: 'I am loath to hold up a still target for the critic'; he is also loath to still his life.[14] Like the Dream Songs, *History* is open-ended, open to revision and extension.

For both Lowell and Berryman poetry becomes appropriative as it becomes a means of survival. Like Bishop's Crusoe, they must endure through gathering and making use of whatever comes their way. Thus *History* and the Dream Songs use and assimilate various sources: both luck and chance contribute to their making. It is unlikely that all of the allusions in *History* and the Dream Songs could ever be traced, since so many are taken from obscure sources or from ephemera. The Dream Songs encompass an astonishing range of learned and other sources – indeed, Berryman once considered the possibility of having notes to the Songs.[15] What is especially striking about the appropriations made by Berryman and Lowell is that they seem entirely opportunistic, seem not to have been chosen with the extreme care that, for example, T. S. Eliot took to ensure that his acknowledged sources contributed structurally and thematically to *The Waste Land*. Dream Song no. 15 ('Let us suppose, valleys & such ago') was originally an anecdote told to Berryman by Saul Bellow, but Berryman would certainly have known of the comparable situation in Nashe's *Unfortunate Traveller*, and his words clearly echo those of Nashe.[16] Joel Conarroe points out that the phrase 'Thick chests quit' in the third Dream Song derived indirectly from an article that Berryman had read in *Life*.[17] Many more examples might be given; the point here is that such appropriations are lucky, opportunistic; 'Luck threw up the coin and the plot swallowed.' One critic pointed out that a poem from *History* is indebted to an editorial from *Commentary*; another that two poems use paraphrases from a piece of art criticism.[18]

That these books are both creation and assimilation is recognised by Lowell in the first of the *History* poems for Berryman:

> I feel I know what you have worked through, you
> know what I have worked through – we are words;
> John, we used the language as if we made it.
> Luck threw up the coin, and the plot swallowed,
> monster yawning for its mess of potage.
> Ah privacy, as if we had preferred mounting
> some rock by a mossy stream and counting the sheep . . . .
> to fame that renews the soul but not the heart.
> The out-tide flings up wonders: rivers, linguini,
> beercans, mussels, bloodstreams; how gaily they gallop
> to catch the ebb – Herbert, Thoreau, Pascal,
> born to die with the enlarged hearts of athletes at forty –
> Abraham sired with less expectancy,
> heaven his friend, the earth his follower.

Of all the revisions which Lowell made to *Notebook*, perhaps the most striking occurs here. Lowell had originally published the poem with the phrase 'these are words, John': the implication being that those words were self-consciously inadequate to the praise he wished to give Berryman. But this later 'we are words' creates a fresh range of ideas. Published after Berryman's death, the poem now further stresses the affinity between *History* and the Dream Songs, and in particular highlights how both books create a life in language. A sense of the transience of such expression is also present, since words and lives are so time-bound.

Like Crusoe, Lowell makes use of random flotsam: 'the out-tide flings up wonders: rivers, linguini, beercans, mussels, bloodstreams . . .'. Lowell fails to provide a single register in which these phenomena may fit. Their individuality and their chance association are not denied, in spite of their incorporation into 'plot'. For though the plot has 'swallowed', 'luck' is always there to regurgitate and introduce fresh phenomena which the plot must then try again to assimilate. The plot cannot be fixed or static; it always has to be ready to swallow, to be able to digest the things thrown up by chance. *History* itself is not fixed as plot. The revisions from which the book is made are evasions, but they also represent temporary plots. The book, Lowell suggests, must be open-ended and open to revision, since the 'out-tide' will always fling up 'wonders'. In a similar way, the plots of history are never fixed, in that fresh events demand or make available fresh perspectives on the past. Lowell once more stresses the association between art and historiography.

In this poem for Berryman, Lowell highlights those qualities that *History* shares with the Dream Songs: thus, here is another of those points in *History* where Lowell is presenting a perspective on his own book. The refusal to be fixed, to 'hold up a still target for critics', has by now become common to Berryman and Lowell. Lowell revises and avoids 'fixing' his own work: Berryman leaves the Dream Songs available for future development, refutes the idea of a consistent identity in the songs, and even suggests that they are not intended to be understood: 'These Songs are not meant to be understood, you understand. / They are only meant to terrify & comfort' (Dream Song 366).

This need to evade fixed meaning is very strong throughout *History*, and it emerges very powerfully in the book's last poem, 'End of a Year':

> These conquered kings pass furiously away;
> gods die in flesh and spirit and live in print,
> each library a misquoted tyrant's home.
> A year runs out in the movies, must be written
> in bad, straightforward, unscanning sentences –
> stamped, trampled, branded on backs of carbons,
> lines, words, letters nailed to letters, words, lines –
> the typescript looks like a Rosetta stone . . .
> One more annus mirabilis, its hero *hero demens*,
> ill-starred of men and crossed by his fixed stars,
> running his ship past sound-spar on the rocks . . .
> The slush-ice on the east bank of the Hudson
> is rose-heather in the New Year sunset;
> bright sky, bright sky, carbon scarred with ciphers.

The poem looks back at *History* and beyond it, in the way that the 'end of a year' is also a new year. Here there is a highly ambiguous attitude towards human attempts to establish an epistemological system and so give meaning to the world. While Lowell recognises that language, most basic and powerful of all human systems, can never define the object, he also sees the attempt to organise and define as a vital human desire. In many respects he seems to end by condemning his own book as a code or system that purports to interpret the world but, in being a code or system, must remain separate from it. Such is the force behind the polarisation of the bright sky and the carbon scarred with ciphers. His book is the carbon, part of an arrangement that cannot define reality. But the sky is also like the new year, the clean slate, the *tabula rasa* momentarily unscarred by interpretation, by all the words that in a year's time will seek to define it and place it in the patterns formed by other years. The clear sky is thus a source of opportunity, indicating the freedom and necessity of human ordering, although it is also representative of what the humanly made system cannot apprehend.

A deeply ambivalent attitude to art, historiography and knowledge, recurring throughout *History*, is most fully expressed here. The human needs to make sense of the world, and the impulses to preserve and assess are examined by Lowell in the opening lines. These are also the impulses behind the making of *History*, as the desire to make things 'live in print' has of course been one of the traditional features of the sonnet sequence. But Lowell's sequence ends finally with a sense of privation and powerlessness. The opposition between the sky and the carbon scarred with ciphers indicates the failure of language to possess and arrest reality. It is an ambivalent attitude because Lowell recognises the need and the instinct to order reality and at the same time he emphasises the impossibility of so doing. The ambivalence is also expressed in 'Fishnet', the marvellous first poem in *Dolphin*, in which the book is self-consciously compared to a fishnet from which the living fish have been lost. But the net remains as a kind of triumphant achievement in itself:

> Yet my heart rises, I know I've gladdened a lifetime
> knotting, undoing a fishnet of tarred rope;
> the net will hang on the wall when the fish are eaten,
> nailed like illegible bronze on the futureless future.

In 'End of a Year' Lowell suggests that behind the creation of history, of art, of human patterns, there is a terrible fear of loss. The year has to be 'written' up out of fear that it will be lost – it must somehow be made to 'live in print'. Throughout *History* there has been the recognition that under the impulse to preserve lies the fear of dispossession. It was suggested above that this was so in the earlier work of Berryman and Lowell, but in *History* and the Dream Songs they face change and loss more fully. On the one hand they both present strategies for dealing with loss – the 'rhetoric of destitution' or the 'epistemology of loss', but they also use deprivation as a theme, and as something which undermines their books, their arrangements. Lowell reminds us that history is absence, 'what you cannot touch'. Berryman reminds us that Anne Bradstreet has been made from the imagination and 'won't stay'. In Elizabeth Bishop's poem, Crusoe the maker will leave his artefacts to the local museum; but the poem ends with his grief over the loss of Friday. However, loss is also the impulse behind creation; Lowell's dismantled rubble is also the material from which fresh things may be built. The 'bright sky' represents possibility as well as failure. The Dream Songs are almost founded on losses; loss of the father being the primary one, the paradigm for all of the other losses that the book considers. But loss or absence is also the paradigm for creation and creativity. Crusoe's shipwreck both necessitates and stimulates his inventiveness. In his poem 'Rhetoric of a Journey' Roy Fuller writes of 'the world / Of art, where something is always missing', and the association between art and loss becomes crucial for Berryman's Dream Songs.

One can deal fairly briefly with the most basic and obvious similarities between *History* and the Dream Songs. Lowell and Berryman both revised extensively the structure and overall concept of their works. Lowell, as outlined above, did so by continual revision of the individual poems and by altering the kind of sequence in which they might eventually be placed. William Meredith suggests that Berryman often had little idea of how any individual song would be situated in the overall sequence; indeed, there is little evidence to suggest that Berryman considered the songs as an arranged sequence.[19] Overall structure appears to have been completely improvisational, and dependent on the songs already written, rather than, for example, Berryman deciding beforehand what kinds of songs would be needed at which points of the sequence. There is a difference here between Lowell's writing daily and then revising with a strong sense of overall structure, since from the start, Lowell had an idea of a basic structure, even if this was as basic as 'Notebook of a Year'. Berryman, though, seemed to write individual songs or small quite compact groups of songs and then try to place them within the existing structure. It seems apparent that for him the larger structure was of less importance than how small sets of the songs might work. Thus critics have usually been able to accept the success of small related sequences while being rather puzzled at their relation to an overall sequence. Some parts of the Dream Songs were quite strongly connected; for example, the *Op. Posth.* section (nos 78–91), and the ten songs – the 'solid block of agony' – on the death of Delmore Schwartz, which open Book VI. At times Berryman also tended to tease those who sought an order in the Songs, suggesting for example, that some parts were arranged in alphabetical order.[20] He once generalised about the Songs, saying that the first 384 are about his father's death while the final one is about his daughter's pregnancy.[21] This is minimally helpful in suggesting, even in the broadest terms possible, a thematic sequence to the Songs. But generally, Lowell and Berryman sought, at different times, different structures for their material.

In part this need for a flexible open structure derived from the obsession which Berryman and Lowell developed for the forms which they had chosen. Lowell apologised for the fact that he 'couldn't stop writing', and Berryman too had a similar problem. Having published *77 Dream Songs* he was quoted in the newspapers as saying that there would be 161 in all.[22] (Actually, it should be noted that what was then Song number 161 remained the last one, eventually numbered 385. It was published in *The Times Literary Supplement* late in 1965, and circulated in pamphlet form to friends of the Berrymans at Christmas that year; on each occasion it bore the title 'The Last Dream Song'.) However, Berryman found that he was unable to stop writing, both in the form and about Henry. 'We asked to be obsessed with writing, / and we were.' As early as 1963 Berryman was complaining in letters that he wanted to finish the Songs because he felt 'self-trapped', and needed freedom to get on with other work.[23] In 1969 he was still obsessed. Although he had said after the publication of *His Toy, His Dream, His Rest* that he was now finished with Henry, Richard Kostelanetz noticed that Berryman had next to him another Dream Song.[24] Of course, he never could let Henry rest, and did not stop writing Dream Songs. He even considered another book of them, to be called either *Addenda* or *Parerga*. Some of these further Dream Songs appeared in the posthumous collection *Henry's Fate* (1977).

Other basic similarities between the Dream Songs and *History* have been suggested already, including the kinds of appropriation that the writing enacts. More importantly, though, the collections are analogous in that Lowell's imaginative creation of history through the self is comparable to Berryman's own creation of order through self. Or rather, through selves, since Henry's identity is flexible. I suggested above that Berryman's view of 'The Ball Poem' as important because it showed him how a 'commitment of identity' could be 'reserved' did not seem especially relevant to that poem. But it is tremendously relevant to the Dream Songs. For as Henry talks of himself in different persons and voices, as Henry himself is changed or his name is changed, his identity is being reserved. It is true that there are some – indeed, many, correspondences between events in Henry's literary existence and events in the real life of Berryman. It is also true that in the later songs Berryman and Henry appear to merge more fully. But Henry is always a persona, through which Berryman's own identity is being reserved. He is a self-consciously fictionalised persona, too, and the very Protean quality of his character ought to remind the reader that Henry is a fiction. His flexible identity is the result of artifice:

> I am an actual human being; Henry is nothing but a series of conceptions – my conceptions. I brush my teeth . . . he doesn't brush his teeth. He only does what I make him do. If I have succeeded in making him believable, he performs all other kinds of actions besides those named in the poem, but the reader has to make them up.[25]

Berryman is in part being playful here, but the point that he makes is important. The association which readers and critics quite naturally make or seek between Henry and Berryman is false, since they fail to take into account the purely fictive status of Henry. At times he is a kind of twentieth-century Everyman, at times only Henry, at times he is dead, at times he assumes different roles. In Dream Song no. 242, which begins 'About that "me"', and is a first person narrative, Henry can end by saying 'I am her' precisely because of his personal flexibility, related in this song to his capacity for absorbing the secret griefs of others into himself.

Of course other issues are raised here. For Berryman, Henry is an artificial construct, but for Berryman personally this would seem to be exactly where his value lies. If Henry's identity is a matter of artifice, then so is Berryman's own. We are returning here to what has been a feature of so much twentieth-century writing: the idea that one's life is like a text that one writes. Each person may be considered an author and the text is the individual's life. Hayden Carruth puts this idea very well; when writing on Lowell he relates Lowell's making of a text to the making of a life:

> A life is what we make it. In its authenticity it is our own interpretation and re-organization of experience, structured metaphorically. It is the result of successive imaginative acts – it is a work of art.[26]

Carruth's emphasis here derives from existentialism: that we each freely construct our lives from various available options, and it is bad faith to allow others to form choices for us. There are clear parallels between making a life as an existentialist series of actions and the artist making a work of art. However, an association between the life and the art-work need not be existentialist in either derivation or emphasis. Throughout the Dream Songs there are references to the idea that a life is analogous to a book. The dead Henry has 'come to a full stop' (no. 85); in the penultimate Dream Song the suicide of Henry's father is comparable to the act of tearing out a page from a book; Henry fearing death in Dream Song no. 112 begins 'My framework is broken, I am coming to an end'; and he later calls himself a 'half-closed book'. These are not only references to a fictive structure that is Henry; they also imply a way of seeing life. Lowell's *History* becomes a creation of history, and placed in such a context his belief '*if I stop* [*writing*]/*I might as well stop breathing*' achieves a special power. In *History* and the Dream Songs the lives of Lowell and Berryman do become textually created fictions, and again this is recognised by Lowell when he writes to Berryman 'we are words'.

But when Henry's identity is inconsistent, and when Berryman even tries to evade the association between himself and Henry, one might ask how Berryman can find Henry so important to him. However, it seems to me that Henry is important precisely because he can change, because he is a created artefact. Henry is not fixed for Berryman, just as history is unsettled for Lowell – it is that capacity to change, indeed, the very need to change, which is at the heart of their strategies for survival. In his notebook Berryman wrote 'Study the creation epics . . . but [the Dream Songs] is a survival-epic.' Being about Henry's survival, it represents Berryman's survival. A fresh thrust is given to the familiar analogy between a life and a text, since Berryman can survive through the creation of an alternative text, or series of texts. Henry's life is of course really a text; so if he comes to a 'full stop' his existence will be completed. Berryman's too? 'Well, mostly I'm through with Henry, but the minute I say that, pains course through me.'[27]

Of course, the songs are about loss as well as survival, and, as with *Life Studies*, about loss making survival necessary. The loss of the father becomes for Henry the basis of the other losses in the songs. Gary Arpin points out that Henry is both 'fatherless' and 'Fatherless'; that the loss of the father brings Henry to experience the loss of belief in God.[28] Critics have also pointed out how the fall which is introduced in the first songs is somewhat redeemed through the attitude Henry has achieved in the final song, an attitude in which he can affirm deprivation:

> Fall is grievy, brisk. Tears behind the eyes
> almost fall. Fall comes to us as a prize
> to rouse us toward our fate.

Berryman can here pun on 'fall' as autumn, which in the context of this song suggests fruition and fulfilment. It is an analogy that Berryman, like Crusoe, is forced to earn, and among all the other things with which the Songs are about, they deal with the problem of how this view of fall as beneficial can be achieved. However, the affirmation of this final song is far from total. Henry's daughter is pregnant, and in the pregnancy Henry finds the affirmation that the songs have sought. But there are some necessary qualifications to be made:

> If there were a middle ground between things and the soul
> or if the sky resembled more the sea,
> I wouldn't have to scold
>   my heavy daughter.

We assume that the daughter needs to be scolded since the coming child will be illegitimate; Berryman's own comment tends to confirm this assumption.[29] In spite of the affirmation evident here, the pregnancy has certainly not lessened a sense of the world's alienation from God, the conflict between 'things and the soul'. The song is set at Thanksgiving, and although it is in a sense an act of thanks, Henry cannot forget even the death that the holiday entails: as if his well-established capacity for feeling the suffering of others has here been extended to sympathy for the sacrificial turkeys. Also the poem begins and ends punningly, with serious playing on the words 'heavier' and 'heavy'. Such play indicates at once the daughter's pregnancy and the grief that the pregnancy has caused, and suggests also the sorry world into which the child will be born.

So, like Lowell in *Life Studies*, Berryman moves towards the positive but finally provides only a limited affirmation. When looking at 'Skunk Hour' I suggested that Lowell's deeper affirmative source was his ability momentarily to transform reality through language, or to read the world and give provisional meaning to it. In a similar way, the affirmations of the Dream Songs rely upon an ability to give a shape and provisional meaning to the world. This idea is related to the concept that Henry is important to Berryman because he is an artefact and has a mutable identity; 'He only does what I make him do.' Behind this mutability is loss and the need to make ways of dealing with loss. It is almost a paradox. Because of loss, because of the fall in the first songs, Henry must evolve a strategy for survival. Yet the quality of his survival derives ultimately from that loss, since privation stimulates his ability to create, to give a provisional meaning to the world:

> Hunger was constitutional with him,
> women, cigarettes, liquor, need, need, need
> until he went to pieces.
> The pieces sat up & wrote. They did not heed
> their piecedom but kept very quietly on
> among the chaos.

> (Dream Song no. 311)

Berryman is said to have greatly admired Ransom's poem 'Captain Carpenter', the poem in which the sad captain is methodically stripped first of his belongings and then of his very limbs.[30] I would suggest that in the Dream Songs the basis of that admiration becomes very clear. For Captain Carpenter is not a victim of loss, rather he is robbed; and Henry too is dispossessed in the Dream Songs. But the more he is stripped, the more he becomes able to cope and survive. Thus the first three books of the Songs end in the seventy-seventh song with Henry 'stript down to move on'. It is the most striking movement of the songs. For, as Henry is stripped, possibilities are open to him, in a way that comes close to Lowell's finding both anguish and renewal in the 'bright sky' at the end of *History*. It is a movement, I feel, which both writers share with Wallace Stevens. For when Stevens finds an openness that is beyond images, a reality which is also nothing, that discovery becomes at once the death of the imagination and the source of its renewal. The 'latest freed man' will move back to find comfort in images; the 'man on the dump' has gone to seek fresh images as the old are in need of renewal. The 'rubble' of Lowell's nihilist is available for rebuilding; Henry is 'stript down' and 'making ready to move on'. He even dies in the songs that immediately follow: the Op. Posth. sequence that Lowell admired most of all. There, the idea of Henry as artefact created by Berryman is most prominent, as is also the idea of Henry the survivor. It is survival achieved through artifice and image-making.

5

Defeats and Dreams

we are words;
John, we used the language as if we made it.

(Lowell, 'For John Berryman 1')

the human

Reverie is a solitude in which
We compose these propositions, torn by dreams,

By the terrible incantations of defeats
And by the fear that defeats and dreams are one.

(Stevens, 'Men Made out of Words'.)

Memory should not be called knowledge.

(Keats to Reynolds, 19 February 1818)

In their final works Randall Jarrell, Elizabeth Bishop and Theodore Roethke firmly consolidated their previous achievements. Some of their finest poetry is in these books: Jarrell's *The Lost World* (1965), Roethke's *The Far Field* (1964), and Bishop's *Geography III* (1976). There can be no doubt that these books confirm the high reputation of the authors, and are entirely consistent with their overall achievement. True, Jarrell's poems in *The Lost World* are more overtly personal than much of his previous work, but all the same, this does not represent a radical new departure for him.

The decline of Delmore Schwartz after the immense promise of his early work has become a familiar story of twentieth-century American poetry. This story has become well known through James Atlas' biography of Schwartz, and through *Humboldt's Gift*, the novel by Saul Bellow. The decline is certainly there, though excessive emphasis on it may blind one to some of the positive qualities of Schwartz's later poetry. Berryman's *Love & Fame* (1970) and Lowell's *Day by Day* (1977) have also been considered as evidence of decline, of loss of talent. These books caused particular problems for reviewers, critics and readers. Neither work was readily accepted into the author's established canon; both were seen as representative of a decline in talent and vision. It is only fairly recently that these attitudes have begun to be questioned as regards *Day by Day*, with critics examining how it is a particular development from some central aspects of Lowell's preceding work. Vereen Bell's book *Robert Lowell: Nihilist as Hero* is important in the perspective it provides on Lowell's career and on *Day by Day*, arguing that this book confirms a pessimism present in all of Lowell's poetry. *Love & Fame*, along with Berryman's posthumously published *Delusions Etc.*, still provokes a negative critical response.

However, like *Day by Day*, *Love & Fame* is at once a consolidation and a development. It consolidates some of the ideas that originated in the Dream Songs yet also moves away from the Songs in an entirely fresh direction. *Love & Fame* and *Day by Day* are challenges to the reader. Berryman and Lowell, as they had done throughout their careers, were keen to explore the possibilities of fresh styles, and did not hesitate to take risks. Again, this willingness to change and impose fresh demands on themselves – and on their readers – is characteristic of them. Berryman's own belief in the worth of *Love & Fame*, a belief shared by Lowell, has been considered suspect by critics who believe that he was reacting too strongly to liberation from Dream Song style. In finding release from his well-established original idiom, they suggest, Berryman too eagerly took up the possibilities that were opened up by a simpler surface texture, and a more straightforward idiom than that offered in the *Sonnets*, *Homage* and the Dream Songs. *Day by Day* was at first received with a kind of respectful hostility. Or rather, respect tempered hostility; Lowell's death only a few weeks after its first (American) publication, clearly made reviewers less unfavourable towards it than they would otherwise have been. Donald Hall, though, made a severe attack on the book, and in doing so he voiced a major complaint against it. Hall was 'depressed by its trashiness', and suggested that its overall tone proclaimed 'the lassitude and despondency of self-imitation'. He concluded that the book would remain 'a sad footnote to the corruption of a great poet'.[1]

Love & Fame had been given much more hostile reviews on its American publication in 1970. Critics attacked it with charges of egotism, vanity and sexual braggadocio; charges particularly relevant to the first parts of the book. It is true that an inflated ego is present in those parts, and the memories offered to us by Berryman are mostly concerned with sexual desire and gratification, in a manner that allows no conventional distance between himself and the narrator. Berryman was very upset by such attacks. For the later English edition of the book in 1971, he excluded or revised the 'worst' poems and issued an 'Afterword' lamenting the evident critical failure to understand the book.

There is a good deal of justice in the attacks on *Love & Fame*. There is an exaggerated interest in self and in sexual conquest; there are parts which seem boastful. But perhaps the failure of critics was in viewing these parts as the essence of the book, whereas they operate in a context allowing strong development. Perhaps such failure to see the book as a sequence is rather surprising, given that Berryman's four previous books (*Homage, 77 Dream Songs, His Toy, His Dream, His Rest* and *Sonnets*) all achieved their finest effects through being considered as sequences. Critics were misled into viewing *Love & Fame* as a series of fairly self-sufficient poems. In the 1971 'Afterword' Berryman showed his pain at such misunderstanding, and was careful to suggest that the poems belonged to an overall structure. For, far from being egotistical, obsessed with self, the direction of the book is away from the self. It begins with the word 'I' but ends with the word 'witness' – Berryman has progressed from a self-involved obsession to what amounts to an effacement of self, a prayer that his life be acceptable finally as a life of witness. The self-interest and concern with lust are there in the first parts but are gradually undermined and seen to be worthless as the book develops. In fact, for apprehension of its power and achievement *Love & Fame* relies far more than Berryman's other works on an understanding of its progression and development.

So, the book's sequence is directed away from the self, and undermines the concepts and worth of love and fame. Critics have speculated a little on Berryman's use of sources in the title, and among the favoured contenders are pieces by Dryden, Keats and Shelley. It should be noted that the title, which of course becomes ironic, does not rely on external reference for its irony. That comes from the book's own plot, as well as from the first parts, where love is lust and achieved fame is expressed in the self-regarding egotism behind all of the poems. Thus the book begins with an apparent equation of love with lust; 'I fell in love with a girl. / O and a gash.' However, as the book develops Berryman prays for the capacity to distinguish between love and lust:

> guard me
> against my flicker of impulse lust: teach me
> to see them as sisters and daughters.

Perhaps the most valid choice for the reference most relevant to the title *Love & Fame* would be that from Keats' sonnet 'When I Have Fears that I may Cease to Be'. As Keats confronts time and death he recognises that love and fame are meaningless:

> then on the shore
> Of the wide world I stand alone and think
> Till love and fame to nothingness do sink

I prefer this since it accurately suggests the idea that for Berryman too love and fame are in the process of becoming worthless. He realises that his understanding of love is imperfect, and that fame is meaningless when compared with the need to be a 'witness' of God's presence. As Berryman rediscovers faith in *Eleven Addresses to the Lord* he establishes a sense of progression not only in *Love & Fame* but in his whole work. In the Dream Songs Henry's loss of his father is concomitant to loss of faith. Both losses form the basis of Henry's 'fall' and his consequent experiences and dilemmas. In *Eleven Addresses* Berryman makes that association more personal and more explicit:

> my father's blow-it-all when I was twelve
> blew out my most bright candle faith, and look at me.

However, there is also reparation: 'I fell back in love with you, Father.' Thus Berryman has come to repair or resolve what Henry never could, and this reparation is made through fresh understanding of love, gained partly through Berryman's earned ability to distinguish love from lust.

As Berryman makes reparation, as he finds a new understanding of love and fame, he also comes to question the ordering principle of the first parts of *Love & Fame*. This questioning, again, is relevant not only to *Love & Fame* as a sequence but also to the development of Berryman in his works. In the Dream Songs Berryman was left with an ambiguous belief in poetry's power to order reality. Through a persona he can order, create self; at the same time he suggests the breakdown of larger human structures of understanding and knowledge. What and how one knows are central problems in *History* and the Dream Songs:

> In his complex investigations of death
> he called for a locksmith, to burst the topic open
> where so many friends have gone . . .

(Dream Song no. 335)

But there are no keys, no answers for Henry. In *Love & Fame* and *Day by Day* Berryman and Lowell come to rely increasingly upon memory as a means of ordering the self. Both books explore the relationship between past and present in highly personal terms, thus expressed as the relation between memory and self. It is as though Berryman and Lowell have gradually contracted, until personal memory is at the centre of knowledge; as though when the other, larger, systems are invalidated memory is still there as a potential arrangement. But there is also a crucial difference, and this difference is indicative of the great difference that finally emerges between Berryman and Lowell. In *Love & Fame* Berryman holds authority over memories. He is, literally in this case, their author. Out of memory he selects, arranges and makes poetry in the first three parts of the book. This selection is made very self-consciously, in three ways. First, the memories are arranged in an overall structure so that they become meaningful. Secondly, Berryman's voice is continually present, often in the present tense, thus reminding the reader that these memories are mediated and selected. Thirdly, Berryman explicitly refers to his control over memory:

> I am not writing an autobiography-in-verse, my friends.
>
> Impressions, structures, tales, from Columbia in the Thirties
> & the Michaelmas term at Cambridge in '36
> followed by some later. It's not my life.
> That's occluded and lost.

('Message')

However, in *Day by Day* Lowell does not direct memory in this manner. He emphasises its involuntary nature, its power of disturbing, of refusing to be repressed, or to provide only that for which it is asked. Berryman is the self-conscious author of the memories in his book, but Lowell, it seems, considers himself more the product of memory. 'I pray for memory' Lowell begins in 'Turtle', but the memories that return are threatening and reductive. Lowell cannot lose his memories and they threaten to destroy him. 'You've wondered where we were these years?' ask the turtles that come unbidden to the surface of Lowell's mind – 'Here we are'. Berryman's reminiscences are controlled and carefully presented so that their menace is removed. Lowell's are associative, involuntary, and continually intimidating.

What does this difference suggest? Berryman's memories take their places eventually in a structure which actually impairs their significance. He places himself at the centre of three parts of *Love & Fame*, but then erases the self, undermines this centre, with *Eleven Addresses*. He implies that through memory and control of memory an order to one's life may be identified or created. It may be a minimal and scarcely adequate order, but it is possible. But then Berryman seeks to delete or reject this minimal human order in favour of the higher order which is provided by God. While the book's first parts are organised around the self, the book's overall structure implies or even enacts a repudiation of such organisation. Berryman controls memory but then relinquishes it in an act of selflessness. Absorption in the self, through a misunderstanding of love and fame, is severely criticised, and Berryman prays finally for its defeat.

Thus Berryman regulates and finally leaves memory. But Lowell remains obsessed and controlled by memory; unwanted and undesirable memories diminish and menace him. So often in *Day by Day* Lowell is helpless before experience, and this passivity seems to be one result of the inability to arrange memory.

> In the realistic memory
> the memorable must be foregone;
> it never matters,
> except in front of our eyes.
>
> I made it a warning,
> a cure, that stabilized nothing.
> We cannot recast the faulty drama . . .

At the end of this poem, 'Grass Fires', the link between his inability to 'recast' memory and to control the present becomes explicit. A memory of having caused a grass fire comes to Lowell. Although he had managed to extinguish the fire, his real, larger defeat is his failure to extinguish memory itself:

> . . . yet it was I put out the fire,
> who slapped it to death with my scarred leather jacket.
> I snuffed out the inextinguishable root,
> I –
> really I can do little,
> as little now as then,
> about the infernal fires –
> I cannot blow out a match.

If here the inability to control memory is symptomatic, or reflects a larger inability to organise experience, then in 'Turtle' the defeat is even more extreme. These turtles, that come to Lowell's mind unbidden and unwanted, have their power increased by Lowell's guilt:

> They lie like luggage –
> my old friend the turtle . . . Too many pictures
> have screamed from the reel . . . in the rerun,
> the snapper holds on till sunset –
> in the awful instantness of retrospect,
> its beak
> works me underwater drowning by my neck,
> as it claws away pieces of my flesh
> to make me small enough to swallow.

In spite of the different ways that Berryman and Lowell approach memory in their books, for both men memories show that as humans they are sealed within time. A writer can use memory as a means of dominating, mastering, time. Memory's power of recall and association works in a way opposed to the sequential progression of time. But the effect of *Love & Fame* and *Day by Day* is to show how powerful memories indicate that the individual is a victim of time. Maybe this effect is communicated less by any individual poem than by recurring themes. Even as he rediscovers

Christian faith Berryman has difficulty in accepting that humans
may transcend time and death:

> We will all die, & the evidence
> is: Nothing after that.
> Honey, we don't rejoin.

('Message')

However, the will for transcendence is there. Lowell's memories
subjugate him in the way that time does. The fear of being plotted,
of life being patterned, recurs again, and here memories are to form
the basis of that pattern:

> causes for my misadventure, considered
> for forty years too obvious to name,
> come jumbling out
> to give my simple autobiography a plot.

('Unwanted')

In one of his last poems, not included in *Day by Day*, Lowell's
commitment to time, his inability to escape, is most clearly
expressed:

> The east wind carries disturbance for leagues –
> I think of my son and daughter,
> and three stepdaughters
> on far-out ledges
> washed by the dreaded clock-clock of the waves . . .
> gradually rotting the bulwark where I stand.
> Their father's unmotherly touch
> trembles on a loosened rail.

('Summer Tides')[2]

The echoes of 'Dover Beach' are again very strong. As in Arnold's
poem, the waves express an inexorable and inescapable progression
– here also their 'clock-clock' indicates their association with time
and our inability to transcend it. The loosened rail and the gradually
rotting bulwark are emblematic of Lowell's own defeat. Whitman's

'firm rail' in 'Crossing Brooklyn Ferry' formed part of his assurance that time could be thwarted – Lowell's 'loosened rail' suggests the opposite idea. The need to accept a time-bound reality is by now a familiar theme of Lowell's poetry. At first it involved a rejection of the ideas of Ransom and Tate, who believed that poetry could evade the mastery of time. However, it emerges with fresh strength in *Day by Day*, partly because memory, a potential source of liberation from time, becomes instead a feature of our subjugation to it.

Delmore Schwartz once complained of the 'tendency of memory to act when invention fails'.[3] What Schwartz had in mind was his own loss of the imaginative power essential to poetry – when that was in abeyance the memory would take over as a shaping force. The substitution of memory for creativity has been considered a key reason for the decline in Schwartz's poetry. In 1943 he published *Genesis, Book I*. There, memories from Schwartz's childhood were recalled and used of the persona Hershey Green. The book is seriously damaged since Schwartz's interest in self is exaggerated to the point where the quality of the poetry suffers through neglect. This epic of Hershey Green's life got no further than the first book, but Schwartz was indeed haunted by memory destroying invention. This complaint was made in his journal long after *Genesis, Book I* was published. The complaint is also relevant to *Love & Fame* and *Day by Day*, and it was echoed by those critics who considered them to be books of egotistical reminiscence.

Berryman begins by writing memoir, shaped as it is by an overall pattern, but then turns his attention to those things which must be imagined rather than being relevant only to personal experience. As he relinquishes his earlier understanding of love and fame he is also repudiating human attempts to order, so that God's order may be revealed to him. Thus the *Eleven Addresses* begin with an emphasis on God as craftsman, as maker of a world that has order, design and purpose, even if these can only be imperfectly apprehended by human understanding:

Master of beauty, craftsman of the snowflake,
inimitable contriver,
endower of Earth so gorgeous & different from the boring Moon,
thank you for such as it is my gift.

This gap between knowledge and belief, between knowledge of human things and knowledge of God, is emphasised again and again in the Addresses. Berryman seeks the means of knowing God and in doing so he obliterates the memories and ideals of the first parts of *Love & Fame*. 'Chameleons feed on light and air, / Poet's food is love and fame' wrote Shelley – one of the sources suggested for Berryman's title.[4] Further increasing the irony of the title, Berryman's nourishment becomes God's word. His poetry attempts finally to imitate God's order – however imperfectly apprehended – rather than his own:

> Oil all my turbulence as at Thy dictation
> I sweat out my wayward works.
> Father Hopkins said that the only true literary critic is Christ.
> Let me lie down exhausted, content with that.

Thus for Berryman memory is usurped as an ordering principle or a means to knowledge in favour of the imagination necessary to comprehension of God's order and purpose. In *Love & Fame* we see a process in which the memory is substituted for a more imaginative approach to experience. But in *Day by Day* it seems that both memory and the poet's imaginative order are lost. Lowell cannot control or order memory, and in a striking way he is no longer the author and the controller of experience. Again and again in *Day by Day* Lowell is presented as passive victim, victim of age, events, of his own 'vast inaccurate memory'.[5] His poetic gift of the ability to order and select cannot bring him liberation from these things.

> Coleridge,
> the author of *Dejection*,
> thought
> genius is the discovery
> of subjects remote
> from my life.
>
> I cannot read.
> Everything I've written
> is greenish brown,
> as if the words
> refused to sound.
>
> ('Wellesley Free')

The associative, almost rambling technique used in *Day by Day* produced adverse criticism – most severely from Donald Hall. However, one can argue that this technique is entirely consistent with the book's recurring theme of human powerlessness before time and events. The major difference between Schwartz and Lowell here is that Schwartz's defeat was not self-conscious. *Genesis, Book I* is the product of invention stifled by memory: *Day by Day* examines such substitution and considers it in a larger context. Thus the inability to create and invent becomes part of a larger inability to control time and experience.

'Fetus' is perhaps one of the poems in which Lowell's method can most readily be seen in its wider context. The starting point for 'Fetus' is the trial of a Boston doctor for killing a foetus. However, Lowell does not take sides in this controversy, even though it appears to demand moral judgement. Thus Helen Vendler, the most perceptive and favourable critic of *Day by Day*, found the poem unsuccessful, partly because Lowell 'no longer has to hand the moral sureness to condemn or approve the abortion'.[6] But the loss of such moral judgement is involved with the other losses and defeats of *Day by Day*, and these are also consistent with the form and technique of 'Fetus'. In several respects, this negation of the capacity for moral judgement was prefigured in 'Waking Early Sunday Morning', from *Near the Ocean*. Lowell's desire to write a public, relevant, poem is constantly challenged by a sub-text threatening the very value and validity of such public poetry. A close focus on 'Fetus' can help to make these points more forcefully and should illuminate the other ideas of *Day by Day*.

In the first major stage of his career Lowell wrote 'The Holy Innocents', where the deaths of the innocents become symbolic of the place of Christian idealism in the twentieth century. It is a text of knowledge, 'whole knowledge', created by a rigorously unified discourse. Lowell transforms event into symbol. But 'Fetus' is not 'whole' in that way, and the kind of knowledge it provides is very different. Lowell does not give us a unified discourse, or a single register within which associations and connotations have precise values relative to an overall structure. 'Fetus' becomes a text that refuses to be consumed. Irony and symbolism appear as possibilities but are never quite developed. For example, towards the end of the poem Lowell writes of the shops 'bonnetted for Easter'. The potential connotations here, of rebirth and resurrection, could suggest an ironic contrast with the murdered foetus. In another kind of poetry such irony could come to form a central statement, directing the reader's response and judgement. But here it is not quite irony. The effect is dissipated, the irony muted. Lowell only suggests, hints. In this case one could point out that the refusal to develop irony is more apparently a result of Lowell's refusal to offer a moral judgement on the case, since to make irony is to offer such judgement. But it is more than that, because the technique is used elsewhere in *Day by Day*, in poems where the moral and ethical issues are not so pronounced. I would suggest that the refusal to create such irony is part of a larger strategy which may be considered as a willingness to be open to experience rather than allowing it to be shaped by the imagination.

Lowell's refusal to symbolise has a comparable effect and arises, I feel, from a similar concern. One could characterise 'Fetus' by its failure to symbolise objects which would be symbolic in another sort of poetry. Indeed, the whole of *Day by Day* could be characterised thus; Helen Vendler wrote of Lowell's struggle to 'break the icon'.[7] For example, 'Fetus' ends with the girl on the billboard:

> . . . ten years my senior in life;
> she would have teased my father –
> unkillable, unlaid,
> disused as the adolescent tan on my hand.
> She is a model, and cannot lose her looks,
> born a decade too soon for any buyer.

What does the girl's picture symbolise? Lost youth? The human capacity or need to make symbols of beauty? The values of exploitative commercialism (connecting it with the shops in February already decorated for Easter)? Maybe the picture itself becomes a criticism of the symbolic. As a symbol of youth and beauty the girl's absurdity is that she can become 'disused'. Like Stevens' statue of General Du Puy, she has lasted 'unkillable' but through that very endurance she has become disused. If the symbolic itself is an aspect of the human desire to escape from time, then as a symbol she has succeeded. But because of our fundamentally human and inescapable involvement with time she is actually inhuman and absurd. This would be one interpretation, but there are others. Lowell does not crystallise meaning through symbolisation and thus he can suggest the broad complexities of human experience.

The poem works in these ways throughout. There are hints of
irony, of symbols, of connections; the lack of a consistent discourse
is also striking. The poem exists as possibility, and is open to
the range of experience, not severely restricted to a single
interpretation. It is typical of *Day by Day*: Lowell is denying the
power of the poetic imagination to interpret ('I cannot read') or
transform experience. Such denial was evident in 'Water', the first
poem in *For the Union Dead*. Maybe 'denial' is too strong a term, too
negative and therefore misleading. For in accepting time Lowell has
accepted, finally, the apparent powerlessness of the imagination. In
'Epilogue' he returns to Schwartz's sense of conflict between
memory and imagination, and begins with a comparable regret:

> Those blessèd structures, plot and rhyme, –
> why are they no help to me now
> I want to make
> something imagined, not recalled?

But he ends with a celebration of all that he can celebrate, and with a
prayer not for the return of imaginative power but for accuracy.
After he has explored in his career the possibilities offered by the
imagination, Lowell finally comes to a view of art as mimetic at best,
to the idea that it must express our temporal human status:

> Yet why not say what happened?
> Pray for the grace of accuracy
> Vermeer gave to the sun's illumination
> stealing like a tide across a map
> to his girl solid with yearning.
> We are poor passing facts,
> warned by that to give
> each figure in the photograph
> his living name.

In the first poem of *Day by Day* Lowell writes of Ulysses and 'his
impoverished life of myth'. For Lowell, the life of myth had indeed
come to seem impoverished. His early work is suffused with myth:
religious myth, the myth of permanence and the universal. In part
this myth had its roots in modernism, and it came partly from the
beliefs of Ransom and Tate. In addition, of course, it was the result

of Lowell's personal religious faith. But he broke away from this myth; away from religious faith, away from modernism, away from the New Critics. *Life Studies* was that break. There Lowell exchanged the 'impoverished' myth for a more flexible and open attitude towards experience. His poetry after *Life Studies* developed still further away from myth, challenging the myths of order, history and of poetry itself.

In 'Men Made Out of Words' Wallace Stevens writes of humans torn by defeats and dreams; 'And by the fear that defeats and dreams are one.' The will for transcendence over time and material reality which is present in *Lord Weary's Castle* can be seen as both defeat and dream. Lowell may be defeated by time and the world and the defeat becomes involved with dream of transcendence. The same is true of Berryman's early poetry. His attitude to art may be symptomatic of either defeat or dream: both Berryman and Lowell may have been 'haunted by the fear' that their dream was inseparable from their defeat. Like Lowell, Berryman was to reject the transcendent in favour of a heuristic approach to experience. But, unlike Lowell, Berryman comes finally to acknowledge his need of the world of myth, and to seek release from the concerns of the world. That is of course the sequence of *Love & Fame*: from an obsession with worldly values to the attempt to overcome them. He rejects his past commitment to the material and the physical, and attempts to find an order that is higher and more meaningful.

However, such a final division of Berryman and Lowell – Berryman affirming a spiritual reality while Lowell tries to accept that we are 'poor passing facts' – is incomplete and misleading. For all of Lowell's sense that the life of myth is 'impoverished', *Day by Day* fails to provide a powerful affirmation of the release from myth. Again, Vereen Bell's book on Lowell needs to be cited, as the most authoritative study of the nihilism of *Day by Day*, and on how that nihilism pervades Lowell's work. Defeat and dream still haunt *Day by Day*, since freedom from myth does not help in giving consolation for humans as 'poor passing facts'. The book has a tragic quality: Lowell himself considered his poetry 'heartbreaking'.[8] It is tragic in that Lowell's rejection of myth does not result in acceptance of or capacity to endure the defeats of time, the loss of friends, of our own mortality. There is a comparable dilemma in *Love & Fame*. In spite of Berryman's affirmation of a higher, meaningful order there is a sense of failure in the book: as though Berryman's faith has its origin only in rejection of the physical rather than in a gift from God. The impatience is strongly present in *Delusions Etc.*, where it seems to border on hysteria:

> It is plain to me
> *Christ* underwent man & treachery & socks
> & lashes, thirst, exhaustion, the bit, for *my* pathetic &
>   disgusting vices,
> to make this filthy fact of particular, long-after
> faraway, five-foot-ten & moribund
> human being happy. Well, he Has!
> I am so happy I could scream!
> It's *enough*! I can't BEAR ANY MORE.
> *Let this be it.* I've *had* it. I can't wait.

Perhaps Berryman's dream is after all allied to Lowell's defeat. In 'Esthetique du Mal' Stevens wrote:

> The greatest poverty is not to live in a physical world,
> To feel that one's desire is too difficult to tell from despair.

But Lowell and Berryman cannot be so positive about the physical world. In *Love & Fame* and *Delusions Etc.* Berryman's desire does seem close to despair, both borne out of a frustration with the physical. In *Day by Day* Lowell sees both desire and despair as impoverishment, and as 'heartbreaking'.

Notes and References

INTRODUCTION

1. Delmore Schwartz, *Selected Essays* (Chicago: University of Chicago Press, 1978) p. 198.
2. Allan Rodway, *London Magazine*, xx (1981) pp. 52–61.
3. A. Alvarez, 'Introduction' to *The New Poetry* (Harmondsworth: Penguin, 1962, 1964).
4. Charles Altieri, *Enlarging the Temple* (Cranburg, N.J.: Associated University Presses Ltd, 1979) p. 58.
5. Lowell, *Day by Day* (London: Faber, 1977) p. 27.
6. Ibid., p. 121.
7. John Haffenden, *The Life of John Berryman* (London and Boston: Routledge & Kegan Paul, 1982) p. 34.
8. Ian Hamilton, *Robert Lowell* (New York: Random House, 1982) pp. 4–7.
9. Lowell, *Sewanee Review*, LXVII (Autumn, 1959) pp. 557–9.
10. Cooper, *The Autobiographical Myth of Robert Lowell* (Chapel Hill: University of North Carolina Press, 1970) p. 42.
11. John Berryman, *The Freedom of the Poet* (New York: Farrar Straus & Giroux, 1976) p. 323.
12. Steven Axelrod, *Robert Lowell: Life and Art* (Princeton: Princeton University Press, 1978) p. 92; Hamilton, *Robert Lowell*, p. 237.
13. Berryman, *The Freedom of the Poet*, p. 327.
14. Hamilton, *Robert Lowell*, p. 438.
15. Lowell, letter to Berryman, 18 March 1962: in John Berryman Collection, University of Minnesota.
16. Lowell, *New York Review of Books*, II (28 May 1964) p. 3.
17. See Haffenden, *The Life of John Berryman*, p. 355.
18. Lowell, cable to Berryman, September 1966, loc. cit.
19. Lowell, letter to Berryman, November 1966, loc. cit., quoted in Haffenden, *The Life of John Berryman*, p. 343.
20. Lowell, letter to Berryman, 27 December 1970, loc. cit.
21. Richard Kostelanetz, *Massachussetts Review*, XI (1970) p. 344.
22. Berryman, letter to an unidentified correspondent, August 1962; John Berryman Collection.
23. Quoted in Haffenden, *The Life of John Berryman*, p. 319.
24. Berryman to Lowell, 13 September 1963: Houghton Library, Harvard University; quoted in Haffenden, *The Life of John Berryman*, p. 323.
25. Thompson, *New York Review of Books*, XXIV (27 October 1977) p. 15.
26. Minneapolis *Star* (4 May 1965) p. 6.
27. Haffenden, *The Life of John Berryman*, p. 318.
28. Kostelanetz, *Massachussetts Review*, p. 341.
29. R. J. Kelly, *John Berryman: A Checklist* (Metuchen, N.J.: Scarecrow Press, 1972) p. xiii.

30. Lowell, letter to Berryman, September 1968, loc. cit.
31. Lowell, letter to Berryman, 15 March 1959, loc. cit.
32. Lowell, *New York Review of Books*, p. 3.
33. Lowell, letter to Berryman, 18 March 1962, loc. cit.

1 BEGINNING IN WISDOM

1. Joel Conarroe, *John Berryman: An Introduction to the Poetry* (New York: Columbia University Press, 1977) pp. 23–4.
2. Lowell, *Sewanee Review*, LXVII (Autumn, 1959) p. 558.
3. Berryman, *The Freedom of the Poet*, p. 323.
4. Cooper, *The Autobiographical Myth*, p. 42.
5. Hugh B. Staples, *Robert Lowell: The First Twenty Years* (London: Faber, 1962) p. 22.
6. Berryman, *The Freedom of the Poet*, p. 288.
7. Ian Hamilton, *London Magazine* (New Series), IV (1965) p. 95.
8. F. R. Leavis, *Lectures in America* (London: Chatto, 1969) pp. 20–1.
9. Ransom, *Harper's Magazine*, CLXIV (July 1932) pp. 221–2.
10. Tate, *Essays of Four Decades* (Oxford University Press, 1974) p. 559.
11. Ransom, *God Without Thunder* (Hamden CT: Archer Books, 1965 [1930]) p. 140.
12. I. A. Richards, *Principles of Literary Criticism* (London: Kegan Paul, 1928) p. 32.
13. Tate, *Essays*, p. 159.
14. Ibid., p. 164.
15. Ransom, *The World's Body* (New York: Charles Scribner's Sons, 1938) pp. 256–7.
16. Tate, *Essays*, p. 350.
17. Ransom, *God Without Thunder*, pp. 22–3.
18. Ibid., p. 136.
19. Ibid., p. 328.
20. See Tate, *Memories and Essays* (Manchester: Carcanet Press, 1979) pp. 41–2.
21. Robert Graves, *The White Goddess* (New York: Creative Age Press, 1948) pp. 353–4.
22. Gerard Manley Hopkins, *Letters to Robert Bridges* (London: Oxford University Press, 1935, 1970) p. 66.
23. Lowell, *Sewanee Review*, LI (1943) pp. 432–3.

2 TOWARDS A RHETORIC OF DESTITUTION

1. E. C. Stefanik, *John Berryman: A Descriptive Bibliography* (Pittsburgh: University of Pittsburgh Press, 1974) pp. 11, 18.
2. Berryman, *The Freedom of the Poet*, pp. 323–31.
3. Ibid., p. 326.

4. Ibid., pp. 326–7.
5. William Carlos Williams, *In the American Grain* (Norfolk CT: New Directions, 1925) p. 67.
6. Staples, *Robert Lowell*, p. 61.
7. Axelrod, *Robert Lowell*, p. 80.
8. Lowell, 'Note' to *For the Union Dead*.
9. Jarrell, *Poetry and the Age* (London: Faber, 1955, 1973) p. 227.
10. Jarrell, *Kipling, Auden & Co.* (New York: Farrar, Straus and Giroux, 1980) pp. 152–3.
11. *Poetry and the Age*, p. 230.

3 EXCELLENCE AND LOSS

1. Anthony Ostroff, *The Contemporary Poet as Artist and Critic* (Boston: Little, Brown, 1964) p. 108.
2. Thomas Parkinson (ed.) *Robert Lowell: A Collection of Critical Essays* (Englewood Cliffs N.J.: Prentice-Hall, 1968) p. 19.
3. Lowell, *Life Studies* (London: Faber, 1959, 1978) p. 27.
4. Altieri, *Enlarging the Temple*, p. 64.
5. Tate, 'Introduction' to *Land of Unlikeness* (Cummington MA: Cummington Press, 1944).
6. Jarrell, *Poetry and the Age*, p. 231.
7. Jonathan Raban, *Robert Lowell's Poems: A Selection* (London: Faber, 1974) p. 22.
8. *Life Studies*, p. 57.
9. Vereen Bell, *Robert Lowell: Nihilist as Hero* (Cambridge MA: Harvard University Press, 1983) pp. 46–54.
10. *Life Studies*, p. 21.
11. Sartre, *Nausea* (Harmondsworth: Penguin, 1975) pp. 61–2 [tr. Baldick]).
12. Paul Bové, *Destructive Poetics* (New York: Columbia University Press, 1980) p. 23.
13. M. L. Rosenthal, *The New Poets* (New York and London: Oxford University Press, 1967) p. 67.
14. Ostroff, *The Contemporary Poet*, p. 98.

4 HISTORY AND SEDUCTION

1. Lowell, *New York Review of Books*, II (28 May 1964) p. 3.
2. Berryman, *The Freedom of the Poet*, p. 329.
3. Jarrell, *Poetry and the Age*, p. 192.
4. Hamilton, *Robert Lowell*, p. 368.
5. Berryman, *The Freedom of the Poet*, p. 327.
6. Clive James, *At the Pillars of Hercules* (London: Faber, 1979) p. 41.
7. Peter Dale, *Agenda*, XI (1973) p. 74.

8. Frank Kermode, *The Genesis of Secrecy* (Cambridge MA: University of Harvard Press, 1980) p. 144.
9. *Works of Charles Lamb*, ed. MacDonald (London: Dent, 1903) vol. iii, p. 277.
10. Ransom, *The World's Body*, p. 348.
11. Axelrod, *Robert Lowell*, p. 204.
12. Lowell, *The Nation*, clxiv (5 April 1947) p. 401.
13. 'Note' to *History*.
14. *Notebook*, p. 264.
15. Haffenden, *John Berryman: A Critical Commentary* (London: Macmillan, 1980) p. 44.
16. Ibid., p. 88; *The Unfortunate Traveller* (Harmondsworth: Penguin, 1972) p. 336.
17. Conarroe, *John Berryman: An Introduction to the Poetry*, p. 99.
18. Axelrod, *English Language Notes*, xi (1974) pp. 206–9; Branscombe, *English Language Notes*, xv (1977) pp. 119–22.
19. Kelly, *John Berryman: A Checklist*, p. xiii.
20. Quoted J. V. Barbera, *Twentieth Century Literature*, xxii (1976) p. 148.
21. Kelly, *John Berryman*, p. xviii.
22. Minneapolis *Tribune* (4 May 1965) p. 6.
23. Haffenden, *The Life of John Berryman*, p. 318; Barbera, *Twentieth Century Literature*, p. 153.
24. Kostelanetz, *Massachusetts Review*, xi (1970) p. 341; Minneapolis *Tribune* (12 May 1968) p. 1E.
25. Peter Stitt, *Paris Review*, no. 53 (1972) p. 193.
26. Hayden Carruth, *Hudson Review*, xx (1967) p. 443.
27. Kostelanetz, *Massachusetts Review*, xi (1970), p. 341.
28. Gary Q. Arpin, *John Berryman Studies*, i (1975) p. 2.
29. Kelly, *John Berryman*, p. xviii.
30. Ibid., p. xxiv.

5 DEFEATS AND DREAMS

1. Donald Hall, *Georgia Review*, xxxii (1978) pp. 10, 12.
2. *New Review*, iv (1977) p. 3; quoted Hamilton, *Robert Lowell*, pp. 469–70.
3. James Atlas, *Delmore Schwartz: The Life of an American Poet* (New York: Avon Books, 1977) p. 349.
4. Shelley, 'An Exhortation'.
5. 'Marriage', *Day by Day*, p. 69.
6. Helen Vendler, *Part of Nature, Part of Us* (Cambridge MA: Harvard University Press, 1980) p. 169.
7. Ibid., p. 144.
8. Ibid., p. 165.

Index